John Bell

Bell's Edition

The poets of Great Britain complete from Chaucer to Churchill

John Bell

Bell's Edition
The poets of Great Britain complete from Chaucer to Churchill

ISBN/EAN: 9783337328436

Printed in Europe, USA, Canada, Australia, Japan

Cover: Foto ©Thomas Meinert / pixelio.de

More available books at **www.hansebooks.com**

THE POETICAL WORKS

OF

CHA. CHURCHILL.

IN THREE VOLUMES,

WITH THE LIFE OF THE AUTHOR.

The Muse's office was by Heaven design'd
To please, improve, instruct, reform, mankind;
To make dejected Virtue nobly rise
Above the towering pitch of splendid Vice;
To make pale Vice, abash'd, her head hang down,
And, trembling, crouch at Virtue's awful frown---
But if the Muse, too cruel in her mirth,
With harsh reflections wounds the man of worth---
Asham'd, she marks that passage with a blot,
And hates the line where candour was forgot. APOLOGY.

VOL. III.

LONDON:

RINTED UNDER THE DIRECTION OF JOHN BELL,
BRITISH LIBRARY, STRAND,
BOOKSELLER TO HIS ROYAL HIGHNESS
THE PRINCE OF WALES.

1793.

THE POETICAL WORKS

OF

CHARLES CHURCHILL.

VOL. III.

CONTAINING HIS

DUELLIST,	TIMES,
GOTHAM,	INDEPENDENCE,
PROPHECY OF FAMINE,	POETRY PROFESSORS.

Let one poor sprig of bay around my head
Bloom whilst I live, and point me out when dead;
Let it (may Heaven, indulgent, grant that prayer!)
Be planted on my grave, nor wither there;
And when, on travel bound, some rhyming guest
Roams thro' the church-yard whilst his dinner's drest,
Let it hold up this comment to his eyes,
Life to the last enjoy'd, Here Churchill lies;
Whilst, (O what joy that pleasing flattery gives!)
Reading my Works, he cries---Here Churchill lives!
CANDIDATE.

LONDON:

RINTED FOR JOHN BELL, BOOKSELLER TO HIS
ROYAL HIGHNESS
THE PRINCE OF WALES.
1793.

THE DUELLIST.

IN THREE BOOKS.

BOOK I.

The clock struck twelve; o'er half the globe
Darkness had spread her pitchy robe:
Morpheus, his feet with velvet shod,
Treading as if in fear he trod,
Gentle as dews at even-tide, 5
Distill'd his poppies far and wide.
  Ambition, who, when waking, dreams
Of mighty but fantastic schemes,
Who when asleep ne'er knows that rest
With which the humbler soul is blest, 10
Was building castles in the air,
Goodly to look upon and fair,
But, on a bad foundation laid,
Doom'd at return of morn to fade.
  Pale Study by the taper's light, 15
Wearing away the watch of night,
Sat reading, but with o'ercharg'd head
Remember'd nothing that he read.

Starving 'midst plenty, with a face
Which might the court of Famine grace, 20
Ragged, and filthy to behold,
Gray Av'rice nodded o'er his gold.
   Jealousy, his quick eye half clos'd,
With watchings worn, reluctant doz'd;
And, mean distrust not quite forgot, 25
Slumber'd as if he slumber'd not.
   Stretch'd at his length on the bare ground,
His hardy offspring sleeping round,
Snor'd restless Labour: by his side
Lay Health, a coarse but comely bride. 30
   Virtue, without the doctor's aid,
In the soft arms of Sleep was laid;
Whilst Vice, within the guilty breast,
Could not be physic'd into rest.
   Thou bloody Man! whose ruffian knife 35
Is drawn against thy neighbour's life,
And never scruples to descend
Into the bosom of a friend,
A firm fast friend by vice ally'd,
And to thy secret service ty'd, 40
In whom ten murders breed no awe
If properly secur'd from law:
Thou man of Lust! whom passion fires
To foulest deeds, whose hot desires
O'er honest bars with ease make way, 45
Whilst idiot Beauty falls a prey,

And to indulge thy brutal flame
A Lucrece must be brought to shame;
Who dost, a brave, bold sinner, bear
Rank incest to the open air,   50
And rapes, full blown upon thy crown,
Enough to weigh a nation down:
Thou simular of Lust! vain man,
Whose restless thoughts still form the plan
Of guilt, which, wither'd to the root,   55
Thy lifeless nerves cann't execute,
Whilst in thy marrowless dry bones
Desire without enjoyment groans:
Thou perjur'd Wretch! whom falsehood clothes
Ev'n like a garment, who with oaths   60
Dost trifle, as with brokers, meant!
To serve thy ev'ry vile intent,
In the day's broad and searching eye
Making God witness to a lie,
Blaspheming heav'n and earth for pelf,   65
And hanging friends to save thyself:
Thou son of Chance! whose glorious soul,
On the four aces doom'd to roll,
Was never yet with honour caught,
Nor on poor virtue lost one thought;   70
Who dost thy wife, thy children, set,
Thy all, upon a single bet,
Risking, the desp'rate stake to try,
Here and hereafter on a die;

Who, thy own private fortune lost, 75
Dost game on at thy country's cost,
And, grown expert in sharping rules,
First fool'd thyself, now prey'st on fools:
Thou noble Gamester! whose high place
Gives too much credit to disgrace, 80
Who with the motion of a die
Dost make a mighty island fly,
The sums, I mean, of good French gold,
For which a mighty island sold;
Who dost betray intelligence, 85
Abuse the dearest confidence,
And, private fortune to create,
Most falsely play the game of state;
Who dost within the Alley sport
Sums which might beggar a whole court, 90
And make us bankrupts all, if Care,
With good Earl Talbot, was not there:
Thou daring Infidel! whom pride
And sin have drawn from Reason's side;
Who, fearing his avengeful rod, 95
Dost wish not to believe a God;
Whose hope is founded on a plan
Which should distract the soul of man,
And make him curse his abject birth;
Whose hope is, once return'd to earth, 100
There to lie down, for worms a feast,
To rot and perish like a beast;

Who dost, of punishment afraid,
And by thy crimes a coward made,
To ev'ry gen'rous soul a curse   105
Than hell and all her torments worse,
When crawling to thy latter end,
Call on Destruction as a friend,
Choosing to crumble into dust
Rather than rise, tho' rise you must: 110
Thou Hypocrite! who dost profane,
And take the patriot's name in vain,
Then most thy country's foe when most
Of love and loyalty you boast;
Who for the filthy love of gold   115
Thy friend, thy king, thy God, hast sold,
And, mocking the just claim of Hell,
Were bidders found thyself wouldst sell.
Ye Villains! of whatever name,
Whatever rank, to whom the claim   120
Of Hell is certain, on whose lids
That worm which never dies forbids
Sweet sleep to fall, come, and behold,
Whilst envy makes your blood run cold,
Behold, by pitiless Conscience led,   125
So Justice wills, that holy bed
Where Peace her full dominion keeps,
And Innocence with Holland sleeps.

 Bid Terror, posting on the wind,
Affray the spirits of mankind;   130

Bid earthquakes, heaving for a vent,
Rive their concealing continent,
And, forcing an untimely birth
Thro' the vast bowels of the earth,
Endeavour, in her monstrous womb,   135
At once all Nature to entomb;
Bid all that's horrible and dire,
All that man hates and fears, conspire
To make night hideous as they can,
Still is thy sleep, thou virt'ous Man!   140
Pure as the thoughts which in thy breast
Inhabit, and ensure thy rest;
Still shall thy Ayliff, taught, tho' late,
Thy friendly justice in his fate,
Turn'd to a guardian angel, spread   145
Sweet dreams of comfort round thy head.

    Dark was the night, by Fate decreed
For the contrivance of a deed
More black than common, which might make
This land from her foundations shake,   150
Might tear up Freedom from the root,
Destroy a Wilkes, and fix a Bute.

    Deep Horror held her wide domain;
The sky in sullen drops of rain
Forewept the morn, and thro' the air,   155
Which op'ning laid its bosom bare,
Loud thunders roll'd and lightning stream'd;
The owl at Freedom's window scream'd,

The screech-owl, prophet dire! whose breath
Brings sickness, and whose note is death; 160
The church-yard teem'd, and from the tomb,
All sad and silent, thro' the gloom
The ghosts of men in former times,
Whose public virtues were their crimes,
Indignant stalk'd; sorrow and rage 165
Blank'd their pale cheek: in his own age
The prop of Freedom, Hampden there
Felt after death the gen'rous care;
Sidney, by grief, from heav'n was kept,
And for his brother patriot wept: 170
All friends of Liberty, when Fate
Prepar'd to shorten Wilkes's date,
Heav'd, deeply hurt, the heart-felt groan,
And knew that wound to be their own.

 Hail! Liberty! a glorious word, 175
In other countries scarcely heard,
Or heard but as a thing of course,
Without or energy or force:
Here felt, enjoy'd, ador'd she springs,
Far, far beyond the reach of kings; 180
Fresh blooming from our mother Earth,
With pride and joy she owns her birth
Deriv'd from us, and in return
Bids in our breasts her genius burn,
Bids us with all those blessings live 185
Which Liberty alone can give,

Or nobly with that spirit die
Which makes death more than victory.
    Hail those old patriots, on whose tongue
Persuasion in the senate hung,   190
Whilst they the sacred cause maintain'd!
Hail those old chiefs, to honour train'd,
Who spread, when other methods fail'd,
War's bloody banner, and prevail'd!
Shall men like these unmention'd sleep   195
Promiscuous with the common heap,
And (Gratitude forbid the crime!)
Be carried down the stream of time
In shoals, unnotic'd and forgot,
On Lethe's stream like flags to rot?   200
No—they shall live, and each fair name,
Recorded in the book of Fame,
Founded on honour's basis, fast
As the round earth to ages last.
Some virtues vanish with our breath;   205
Virtue like this lives after death.
Old Time himself, his sithe thrown by,
Himself lost in eternity,
An everlasting crown shall twine
To make a Wilkes and Sidney join.   210
    But should some slave-got villain dare
Chains for his country to prepare,
And, by his birth to slav'ry broke,
Make her too feel the galling yoke,

May he be evermore accurst, 215
Amongst bad men be rank'd the worst;
May he be still himself, and still
Go on in vice, and perfect ill;
May his broad crimes each day increase,
Till he cann't live nor die in peace; 220
May he be plung'd so deep in shame
That Satan may n't endure his name,
And hear, scarce crawling on the earth,
His children curse him for their birth;
May Liberty, beyond the grave, 225
Ordain him to be still a slave,
Grant him what here he most requires,
And damn him with his own desires!
But should some villain, in support
And zeal for a despairing court, 230
Placing in craft his confidence,
And making honour a pretence
To do a deed of deepest shame,
Whilst filthy lucre is his aim;
Should such a wretch with sword or knife 235
Contrive to practise 'gainst the life
Of one who, honour'd thro' the land,
For Freedom made a glorious stand,
Whose chief perhaps his only crime
Is, (if plain Truth at such a time 240
May dare her sentiments to tell)
'That he his country loves too well:

May he—but words are all too weak
The feelings of my heart to speak—
May he—O for a noble curse   245
Which might his very marrow pierce!—
The general contempt engage,
And be the Martin of his age!   248

THE DUELLIST.

BOOK II.

Deep in the bosom of a wood,
Out of the road, a temple stood;
Ancient, and much the worse for wear,
It call'd aloud for quick repair,
And tottering from side to side   5
Menac'd destruction far and wide,
Nor able seem'd, unless made stronger,
To hold out four or five years longer.
Four hundred pillars, from the ground
Rising in order, most unsound,   10
Some rotten to the heart, aloof
Seem to support the tott'ring roof,
But to inspection nearer laid
Instead of giving wanted aid.
  The structure, rare and curious made   15
By men most famous in their trade,
A work of years, admir'd by all,
Was suffer'd into dust to fall;
Or, just to make it hang together,
And keep off the effects of weather,   20
Was patch'd and patch'd from time to time
By wretches, whom it were a crime,

A crime which Art would treason hold
To mention with those names of old.
    Builders, who had the pile survey'd,
And those not Flitcrofts in their trade,
Doubted (the wise hand in a doubt
Merely sometimes to hand her out)
Whether (like churches in a brief,
Taught wisely to obtain relief
Thro' Chancery, who gives her fees
To this and other charities)
It must not, in all parts unsound,
Be ripp'd and pull'd down to the ground;
Whether (tho' after ages ne'er
Shall raise a building to compare)
Art, if they should their art employ,
Meant to preserve, might not destroy;
As human bodies worn away,
Batter'd and hasting to decay,
Bidding the pow'r of Art despair,
Cannot those very med'cines bear
Which and which only can restore,
And make them healthy as before.
    To Liberty, whose gracious smile
Shed peace and plenty o'er the isle,
Our grateful ancestors, her plain
But faithful children, rais'd this fane.
    Full in the front, stretch'd out in length,
Where Nature put forth all her strength

In spring eternal, lay a plain
Where our brave fathers us'd to train
Their sons to arms, to teach the art
Of war, and steel the infant heart.
Labour, their hardy nurse, when young, 55
Their joints had knit, their nerves had strung;
Abstinence, foe declar'd to death,
Had, from the time they first drew breath,
The best of doctors, with plain food,
Kept pure the channel of their blood; 60
Health in their cheeks bade colour rise,
And Glory sparkled in their eyes.
   The instruments of husbandry,
As in contempt, were all thrown by,
And, flattering a manly pride, 65
War's keener tools their place supply'd.
   Their arrows to the head they drew;
Swift to the point their jav'lins flew;
They grasp'd the sword, they shook the spear;
Their fathers felt a pleasing fear, 70
And even Courage, standing by,
Scarcely beheld with steady eye.
Each stripling, lesson'd by his sire,
Knew when to close, when to retire;
When near at hand, when from afar 75
To fight, and was himself a war.
   Their wives, their mothers, all around,
Careless of order, on the ground

Breath'd forth to Heav'n the pious vow,
And for a son's or husband's brow, 80
With eager fingers, laurel wove,
Laurel which, in the sacred grove,
Planted by Liberty, they find,
The brows of conquerors to bind,
To give them pride and spirits, fit 85
To make a world in arms submit.

    What raptures did the bosom fire
Of the young, rugged, peasant sire,
When, from the toil of mimic fight,
Returning with return of night, 90
He saw his babe resign the breast,
And, smiling, stroke those arms in jest,
With which hereafter he shall make
The proudest heart in Gallia quake!

    Gods! with what joy, what honest pride, 95
Did each fond, wishing, rustic, bride
Behold her manly swain return!
How did her love-sick bosom burn,
Tho' on parades he was not bred,
Nor wore the livery of red, 100
When, pleasure height'ning all her charms,
She strain'd her warrior in her arms,
And begg'd, whilst love and glory fire,
A son, a son just like his sire!

    Such were the men in former times, 105
Ere luxury had made our crimes

Our bitter punishment, who bore
Their terrors to a foreign shore:
Such were the men who, free from dread,
By Edwards and by Henrys led, 110
Spread, like a torrent swell'd with rains,
O'er haughty Gallia's trembling plains:
Such were the men when lust of pow'r,
To work him wo in evil hour,
Debauch'd the tyrant from those ways 115
On which a king should found his praise;
When stern Oppression, hand in hand
With Pride, stalk'd proudly thro' the land;
When weeping Justice was misled
From her fair course, and Mercy dead: 120
Such were the men, in virtue strong,
Who dar'd not see their country's wrong,
Who left the mattock and the spade,
And, in the robes of war array'd,
In their rough arms, departing, took 125
Their helpless babes, and with a look
Stern and determin'd, swore to see
Those babes no more, or see them free:
Such were the men whom tyrant Pride
Could never fasten to his side 130
By threats or bribes, who, freemen born,
Chains, tho' of gold, beheld with scorn;
Who, free from ev'ry servile awe,
Could never be divorc'd from law,

From that broad gen'ral law which sense   135
Made for the general defence;
Could never yield to partial ties
Which from dependent stations rise;
Could never be to slav'ry led,
For Property was at their head: 140
Such were the men, in days of yore,
Who, call'd by Liberty, before
Her temple on the sacred green
In martial pastimes oft' were seen—
Now seen no longer—in their stead,   145
To laziness and vermine bred,
A race who, strangers to the cause
Of Freedom, live by other laws,
On other motives fight, a prey
To interest, and slaves for pay.   150
Valour, how glorious on a plan
Of honour founded! leads their van;
Discretion, free from taint of fear,
Cool but resolv'd, brings up the rear;
Discretion, Valour's better half;   155
Dependence holds the gen'ral's staff.

    In plain and home-spun garb array'd,
Not for vain show but service made,
In a green flourishing old age,
Not damn'd yet with an equipage,   160
In rules of Porterage untaught,
Simplicity, not worth a groat,

For years had kept the temple-door;
Full on his breast a glass he wore,
Thro' which his bosom open lay   165
To ev'ry one that pass'd that way:
Now turn'd adrift—with humbler face
But prouder heart, his vacant place
Corruption fills, and bears the key;
No entrance now without a fee.   170

   With belly round, and full fat face,
Which on the house reflected grace,
Full of good fare and honest glee,
The steward Hospitality,
Old Welcome smiling by his side,   175
A good old servant, often try'd,
And faithful found, who kept in view
His lady's fame and int'rest too,
Who made each heart with joy rebound,
Yet never run her state aground,   180
Was turn'd off, or (which word I find
Is more in modern use) resign'd.

   Half-starv'd, half-starving others, bred
In beggary, with carrion fed,
Detested and detesting all,   185
Made up of avarice and gall,
Boasting great thrift, yet wasting more
Than ever steward did before,
Succeeded one who, to engage
The praise of an exhausted age,   190

Assum'd a name of high degree,
And call'd himself Economy.
 Within the temple, full in sight,
Where without ceasing day and night
The workman toil'd; where Labour bar'd   195
His brawny arm; where Art prepar'd,
In regular and even rows,
Her types, a Printing-press arose;
Each workman knew his task, and each
Was honest and expert as Leach.   200
 Hence Learning struck a deeper root,
And Science brought forth riper fruit;
Hence Loyalty receiv'd support,
Even when banish'd from the court;
Hence Government gain'd strength, and hence 205
Religion sought and found defence;
Hence England's fairest fame arose,
And Liberty subdu'd her foes.
 On a low, simple, turf-made throne,
Rais'd by Allegiance, scarcely known   210
From her attendants, glad to be
Pattern of that equality
She wish'd to all, so far as cou'd
Safely consist with social good,
The goddess sat; around her head   215
A cheerful radiance Glory spread:
Courage, a youth of royal race,
Lovelily stern, possess'd a place

On her left hand, and on her right
Sat Honour, cloth'd with robes of light; 220
Before her Magna Charta lay,
Which some great lawyer, of his day
The Pratt, was offic'd to explain,
And make the basis of her reign:
Peace, crown'd with olive, to her breast 225
Two smiling twinborn infants prest;
At her feet couching War was laid,
And with a brindled lion play'd:
Justice and Mercy, hand in hand,
Joint guardians of the happy land, 230
Together held their mighty charge,
And Truth walk'd all about at large:
Health for the royal troop the feast
Prepar'd, and Virtue was high priest.

Such was the fame our goddess bore, 235
Her temple such, in days of yore.
What changes ruthless Time presents!
Behold her ruin'd battlements,
Her walls decay'd, her nodding spires,
Her altars broke, her dying fires, 240
Her name despis'd, her priests destroy'd,
Her friends disgrac'd, her foes employ'd,
Herself (by ministerial arts
Depriv'd ev'n of the people's hearts,
Whilst they, to work her surer wo, 245
Feign her to monarchy a foe)

Exil'd by grief, self-doom'd to dwell
With some poor hermit in a cell;
Or, that retirement tedious grown,
If she walks forth she walks unknown, 250
Hooted and pointed at with scorn,
As one in some strange country born.
 Behold a rude and ruffian race,
A band of spoilers, seize her place;
With looks which might the heart disseat, 255
And make life sound a quick retreat,
To rapine from the cradle bred,
A staunch old bloodhound at their head,
Who, free from virtue and from awe,
Knew none but the bad part of law, 260
They rov'd at large; each on his breast
Mark'd with a grayhound * stood confest:
Controlment waited on their nod,
High-wielding Persecution's rod;
Confusion follow'd at their heels, 265
And a cast statesman held the seals;
Those seals for which he dear shall pay,
When awful Justice takes her day.
 The Printers saw—they saw and fled—
Science declining hung her head; 270
Property in despair appear'd,
And for herself destruction fear'd;

---

* The King's messengers bear this emblematical badge of their swiftness.

Whilst under foot the rude slaves trod
The works of men and word of God;
Whilst, close behind, on many a book, 275
In which he never deigns to look,
Which he did not, nay—could not, read,
A bold bad man (by pow'r decreed
For that bad end, who in the dark
Scorn'd to do mischief) set his mark 280
In the full day, the mark of Hell,
And on the Gospel stamp'd an L.

Liberty fled, her friends withdrew—
Her friends, a faithful chosen few;
Honour in grief threw up, and Shame, 285
Clothing herself with Honour's name,
Usurp'd his station: on the throne
Which Liberty once call'd her own,
(Gods! that such mighty ills should spring
Under so great, so good, a king, 290
So lov'd, so loving, thro' the arts
Of statesmen, curs'd with wicked hearts!)
For ev'ry darker purpose fit,
Behold in triumph Statecraft sit. 294

BOOK III.

Ah me! what mighty perils wait
The man who meddles with a state,
Whether to strengthen or oppose!
False are his friends and firm his foes:
How must his soul, once ventur'd in,   5
Plunge blindly on from sin to sin!
What toils he suffers, what disgrace,
To get, and then to keep, a place!
How often, whether wrong or right,
Must he in jest or earnest fight,   10
Risking for those both life and limb
Who would not risk one groat for him!

    Under the temple lay a cave,
Made by some guilty coward slave
Whose actions fear'd rebuke; a maze   15
Of intricate and winding ways,
Not to be found without a clue;
One passage only, known to few,
In paths direct led to a cell,
Where Fraud in secret lov'd to dwell,   20
With all her tools and slaves about her,
Nor fear'd lest Honesty should rout her.

    In a dark corner, shunning sight
Of man, and shrinking from the light,
One dull dim taper thro' the cell   25
Glimm'ring, to make more horrible

The face of darkness; she prepares,
Working unseen, all kinds of snares
With curious but destructive art.
Here, thro' the eye to catch the heart, 30
Gay stars their tinsel beams afford,
Neat artifice to trap a lord;
There, fit for all whom Folly bred,
Wave plumes of feathers for the head;
Garters the hag contrives to make 35
Which, as it seems, a babe might break,
But which ambitious madmen feel
More firm and sure than chains of steel,
Which slipp'd just underneath the knee,
Forbid a freeman to be free. 40
Purses she knew (did ever curse
Travel more sure than in a purse?)
Which by some strange and magic bands
Enslave the soul and tie the hands.

 Here Flatt'ry, eldest born of Guile, 45
Weaves with rare skill the silken smile,
The courtly cringe, the supple bow,
The private squeeze, the levee vow,
With which, no strange or recent case,
Fools in deceive fools out of place. 50

 Corruption (who, in former times,
Thro' fear or shame conceal'd her crimes,
And what she did contriv'd to do it
So that the public might not view it)
       C ij

Presumpt'ous grown, unfit was held 55
For their dark councils, and expell'd,
Since in the day her bus'ness might
Be done as safe as in the night.
   Her eye down-bending to the ground,
Planning some dark and deadly wound, 60
Holding a dagger, on which stood,
All fresh and reeking, drops of blood,
Bearing a lanthorn, which of yore,
By Treason borrow'd, Guy Fawkes bore,
By which, since they improv'd in trade, 65
Excisemen have their lanthorns made,
Assassination, her whole mind
Blood-thirsting, on her arm reclin'd;
Death grinning at her elbow stood,
And held forth instruments of blood, 70
Vile instruments, which cowards choose,
But men of honour dare not use;
Around his Lordship and his Grace,
Both qualify'd for such a place,
With many a Forbes and many a Dun, 75
Each a resolv'd and pious son,
Wait her high bidding; each prepar'd,
As she around her orders shar'd,
Proof 'gainst remorse, to run, to fly,
And bid the destin'd victim die, 80
Posting on Villany's black wing,
Whether he patriot is or king.

Oppression, willing to appear
An object of our love, not fear,
Or, at the most, a rev'rend awe 85
To breed, usurp'd the garb of Law.
A book she held, on which her eyes
Were deeply fix'd, whence seem'd to rise
Joy in her breast; a book of might
Most wonderful, which black to white 90
Could turn, and, without help of laws,
Could make the worse the better cause.
She read, by flatt'ring hopes deceiv'd,
She wish'd, and what she wish'd believ'd,
To make that book for ever stand 95
The rule of wrong thro' all the land;
On the back, fair and worthy note,
At large was Magna Charta wrote,
But turn your eye within, and read,
A bitter lesson, N——'s Creed. 100
Ready, ev'n with a look, to run
Fast as the coursers of the sun,
To worry Virtue, at her hand
Two half-starv'd grayhounds took their stand.
A curious model, cut in wood, 105
Of a most ancient castle stood
Full in her view; the gates were bar'd,
And soldiers on the watch kept guard;
In the front, openly, in black
Was wrote, The Tow'r; but on the back, 110

C iij

Mark'd with a secretary's seal,
In bloody letters, The Bastile.
   Around a table, fully bent
On mischief of most black intent,
Deeply determin'd that their reign   115
Might longer last to work the bane
Of one firm patriot, whose heart, ty'd
To honour, all their pow'r defy'd,
And brought those actions into light
They wish'd to have conceal'd in night,   120
Begot, born, bred, to infamy,
A privy-council sat of three:
Great were their names, of high repute
And favour through the land of Bute.
   The first (entitled to the place   125
Of honour both by gown and grace,
Who never let occasion slip
To take right hand of fellowship,
And was so proud, that should he meet
The Twelve Apostles in the street   130
He'd turn his nose up at them all,
And shove his Saviour from the wall;
Who was so mean (Meanness and Pride
Still go together side by side)
That he would cringe, and creep, be civil,   135
And hold a stirrup for the devil;
If in a journey to his mind
He'd let him mount, and ride behind;

Who basely fawn'd thro' all his life,
For patrons first, then for a wife;   140
Wrote Dedications which must make
The heart of ev'ry Christian quake;
Made one man equal to, or more
Than God, then left him, as before
His God he left, and, drawn by pride,   145
Shifted about to t'other side)
Was by his sire a parson made,
Merely to give the boy a trade;
But he himself was thereto drawn
By some faint omens of the lawn,   150
And on the truly Christian plan
To make himself a gentleman,
A title in which Form array'd him,
Tho' Fate ne'er thought on't when she made him.

   The oaths he took, 'tis very true,   155
But took them, as all wise men do,
With an intent, if things should turn,
Rather to temporize than burn.
Gospel and loyalty were made
To serve the purposes of trade;   160
Religions are but paper ties,
Which bind the fool, but which the wise,
Such idle notions far above,
Draw on and off, just like a glove:
All gods, all kings (let his great aim   165
Be answer'd), were to him the same.

A curate first, he read and read,
And laid in, whilst he should have fed
The souls of his neglected flock,
Of reading such a mighty stock, 170
That he o'ercharg'd the weary brain
With more than she could well contain;
More than she was with spirits fraught
To turn and methodize to thought,
And which, like ill-digested food, 175
To humours turn'd and not to blood.
Brought up to London from the plow
And pulpit, how to make a bow
He try'd to learn; he grew polite,
And was the poet's parasite. 180
With wits conversing (and wits then
Were to be found 'mongst noblemen)
He caught, or would have caught, the flame,
And would be nothing, or the same.
He drank with drunkards, liv'd with sinners, 185
Herded with infidels for dinners;
With such an emphasis and grace
Blasphem'd, that Potter kept not pace;
He, in the highest reign of noon,
Bawl'd bawdy songs to a psalm tune; 190
Liv'd with men infamous and vile,
Truck'd his salvation for a smile;
To catch their humour caught their plan,
And laugh'd at God to laugh with man;

Prais'd them, when living, in each breath, 195
And damn'd their mem'ries after death.
   To prove his faith, which all admit
Is at least equal to his wit,
And make himself a man of note,
He in defence of Scripture wrote: 200
So long he wrote, and long, about it,
That ev'n believers 'gan to doubt it :
He wrote too of the inward light,
Tho' no one knew how he came by 't,
And of that influencing grace 205
Which in his life ne'er found a place :
He wrote too of the Holy Ghost,
Of whom no more than doth a post
He knew, nor, should an angel show him,
Would he or know or choose to know him. 210
   Next (for he knew 'twixt ev'ry science
There was a natural alliance)
He wrote, t' advance his Maker's praise,
Comments on rhymes, and notes on plays,
And with an all-sufficient air 215
Plac'd himself in the critic's chair,
Usurp'd o'er reason full dominion,
And govern'd merely by opinion.
At length dethron'd, and kept in awe
By one plain simple man of law, 220
He arm'd dead friends, to vengeance true,
T' abuse the man they never knew.

Examine strictly all mankind,
Most characters are mix'd we find,
And vice and virtue take their turn, 225
In the same breast to beat and burn.
Our priest was an exception here,
Nor did one spark of grace appear,
Not one dull dim spark, in his soul;
Vice, glorious Vice! possess'd the whole, 230
And, in her service truly warm,
He was in sin most uniform.
 Injurious Satire! own at least
One sniv'ling virtue in the priest,
One sniv'ling virtue, which is plac'd, 235
They say, in or about the waist,
Call'd Chastity, the prudish dame
Knows it at large by Virtue's name.
To this his wife (and in these days
Wives seldom without reason praise) 240
Bears evidence—then calls her child,
And swears that Tom was vastly wild.
 Ripen'd by a long course of years,
He great and perfect now appears.
In shape scarce of the human kind, 245
A man without a manly mind;
No husband tho' he 's truly wed;
Tho' on his knees a child is bred
No father; injur'd, without end
A foe; and tho' oblig'd no friend; 250

A heart, which virtue ne'er disgrac'd;
A head where learning runs to waste;
A gentleman well bred, if breeding
Rests in the article of reading;
A man of this world, for the next 255
Was ne'er included in his text;
A judge of genius, tho' confess'd
With not one spark of genius bless'd;
Amongst the first of critics plac'd,
Tho' free from ev'ry taint of taste; 260
A Christian without faith or works,
As he would be a Turk 'mongst Turks;
A great divine, as lords agree,
Without the least divinity.
To crown all, in declining age, 265
Inflam'd with church and party rage,
Behold him, full and perfect quite,
A false saint and true hypocrite.
 Next sat a lawyer, often try'd
In perilous extremes. When Pride 270
And Pow'r all wild and trembling stood,
Nor dar'd to tempt the raging flood,
This bold bad man arose to view,
And gave his hand to help them thro':
Steel'd 'gainst compassion, as they past 275
He saw poor Freedom breathe her last;
He saw her struggle, heard her groan;
He saw her helpless and alone,

'Whelm'd in that storm, which, fear'd and prais'd
By slaves less bold, himself had rais'd. 280
   Bred to the law, he from the first
Of all bad lawyers was the worst.
Perfection (for bad men maintain
In ill we may perfection gain)
In others is a work of time, 285
And they creep on from crime to crime;
He, for a prodigy design'd
To spread amazement o'er mankind,
Started full ripen'd all at once
A perfect knave and perfect dunce. 290
   Who will for him may boast of sense,
His better guard is impudence:
His front, with ten-fold plates of brass
Secur'd, Shame never yet could pass,
Nor on the surface of his skin 295
Blush for that guilt which dwelt within.
How often, in contempt of laws,
To sound the bottom of a cause,
To search out ev'ry rotten part,
And worm into its very heart, 300
Hath he ta'en briefs on false pretence
And undertaken the defence
Of trusting fools, whom in the end
He meant to ruin, not defend?
How often, ev'n in open court, 305
Hath the wretch made his shame his sport,

And laugh'd off, with a villain's ease,
Throwing up briefs and keeping fees?
Such things as, tho' to rogu'ry bred,
Had struck a little villain dead.
 Causes, whatever their import,
He undertakes to serve a court;
For he by heart this rule had got;
Pow'r can effect what law cannot.
 Fools he forgives, but rogues he fears;
If Genius yok'd with Worth appears,
His weak soul sickens at the sight,
And strives to plunge them down in night.
 So loud he talks, so very loud,
He is an angel with the crowd,
Whilst he makes Justice hang her head,
And judges turn from pale to red.
 Bid all that Nature, on a plan
Most intimate, makes dear to man,
All that with grand and gen'ral ties
Binds good and bad, the fool and wise,
Knock at his heart; they knock in vain;
No entrance there such suitors gain:
Bid kneeling kings forsake the throne,
Bid at his feet his country groan;
Bid Liberty stretch out her hands,
Religion plead her stronger bands;
Bid parents, children, wife, and friends,
If they come thwart his private ends,

Unmov'd he hears the gen'ral call, 335
And bravely tramples on them all.
   Who will for him may cant and whine,
And let weak Conscience with her line
Chalk out their ways; such starving rules
Are only fit for coward fools, 340
Fellows who credit what priests tell,
And tremble at the thoughts of hell;
His spirit dares contend with Grace,
And meets Damnation face to face.
   Such was our lawyer; by his side 345
In all bad qualities ally'd,
In all bad counsels, sat a third,
By birth a lord; O sacred word!
O word most sacred! whence men get
A privilege to run in debt; 350
Whence they at large exemption claim
From Satire, and her servant Shame;
Whence they, depriv'd of all her force,
Forbid bold Truth to hold her course.
   Consult his person, dress, and air, 355
He seems, which strangers well might swear,
The master, or, by courtesy,
The captain, of a colliery.
Look at his visage, and agree
Half-hang'd he seems, just from the tree 360
Escap'd; a rope may sometimes break,
Or men be cut down by mistake.

He hath not virtue (in the school
Of Vice bred up) to live by rule,
Nor hath he sense (which none can doubt   365
Who know the man) to live without.
His life is a continu'd scene
Of all that 's infamous and mean.
He knows not change, unless, grown nice
And delicate, from vice to vice;   370
Nature design'd him in a rage
To be the Wharton of his age,
But having giv'n all the sin,
Forgot to put the virtues in.
To run a horse, to make a match,   375
To revel deep, to roar a catch,
To knock a tott'ring watchman down,
To sweat a woman of the Town;
By fits to keep the peace or break it,
In turn to give a pox or take it,   380
He is, in faith, most excellent,
And, in the word's most full intent,
A true Choice Spirit, we admit,
With wits a fool, with fools a wit.
Hear him but talk, and you would swear   385
Obscenity herself was there,
And that Profaneness had made choice,
By way of trump, to use his voice:
That in all mean and low things great,
He had been bred at Billingsgate;   390

And that, ascending to the earth
Before the season of his birth,
Blasphemy, making way and room,
Had mark'd him in his mother's womb:
Too honest (for the worst of men   395
In forms are honest now and then)
Not to have, in the usual way,
His bills sent in; too great to pay:
Too proud to speak to, if he meets
The honest tradesman whom he cheats;   400
Too infamous to have a friend;
Too bad for bad men to commend,
Or good to name; beneath whose weight
Earth groans; who hath been spar'd by Fate
Only to shew, on mercy's plan,   405
How far and long God bears with man.

 Such were the three who, mocking sleep,
At midnight sat, in council deep,
Plotting destruction 'gainst a head
Whose wisdom could not be misled,   410
Plotting destruction 'gainst a heart
Which ne'er from honour would depart.

 " Is he not rank'd amongst our foes?
" Hath not his spirit dar'd oppose
" Our dearest measures, made our name   415
" Stand forward on the roll of shame?
" Hath he not won the vulgar tribes
" By scorning menaces and bribes,

" And proving that his darling cause
" Is of their liberties and laws   420
" To stand the champion? In a word,
" Nor need one argument be heard
" Beyond this to awake our zeal,
" To quicken our resolves, and steel
" Our steady souls to bloody bent,   425
" (Sure ruin to each dear intent,
" Each flatt'ring hope) he, without fear,
" Hath dar'd to make the truth appear."
They said, and, by resentment taught,
Each on revenge employ'd his thought,   430
Each, bent on mischief, rack'd his brain
To her full stretch, but rack'd in vain:
Scheme after scheme they brought to view;
All were examin'd; none would do:
When Fraud, with pleasure in her face,   435
Forth issu'd from her hiding-place,
And at the table where they meet,
First having bless'd them, took her seat.
" No trifling cause, my darling Boys!
" Your present thoughts and cares employs;   440
" No common snare, no random blow,
" Can work the bane of such a foe;
" By Nature cautious as he's brave,
" To honour only he's a slave;
" In that weak part without defence   445
" We must to honour make pretence:

"The lure shall to his ruin draw
"The wretch who stands secure in law:
"Nor think that I have idly plann'd
"This full-ripe scheme; behold at hand,   450
"With three months training on his head,
"An instrument whom I have bred,
"Born of these bowels, far from sight
"Of virtue's false but glaring light,
"My youngest born, my dearest joy,   455
"Most like myself, my darling boy:
"He, never touch'd with vile remorse,
"Resolv'd and crafty in his course,
"Shall work our ends, complete our schemes,
"Most mine when most he Honour's seems;   460
"Nor can be found, at home, abroad,
"So firm and full a slave of Fraud."
    She said, and from each envious son
A discontented murmur run
Around the table; all in place   465
Thought his full praise their own disgrace,
Wond'ring what stranger she had got
Who had one vice that they had not;
When straight the portals open flew,
And, clad in armour, to their view   470
M——, the Duellist, came forth;
All knew and all confess'd his worth;
All justify'd, with smiles array'd,
The happy choice their dam had made.

GOTHAM.

IN THREE BOOKS.

BOOK I.

Far off (no matter whether east or west,
A real country, or one made in jest,
Not yet by modern Mandevilles disgrac'd,
Nor by map-jobbers wretchedly misplac'd)
There lies an island, neither great nor small,   5
Which for distinction sake I Gotham call.
    The man who finds an unknown country out,
By giving it a name acquires, no doubt,
A Gospel title, tho' the people there
The pious Christian thinks not worth his care: 10
Bar this pretence, and into air is hurl'd
The claim of Europe to the Western world.
    Cast by a tempest on the savage coast,
Some roving buccaneer set up a post;
A beam, in proper form transversely laid,   15
Of his Redeemer's cross t' e figure made,
Of that Redeemer with whose laws his life,
From first to last, had been one scene of strife;
His royal master's name thereon engrav'd,
Without more process the whole race enslav'd,   20
Cut off that charter they from Nature drew,
And made them slaves to men they never knew.
    Search ancient histories, consult records,
Under this title the most Christian lords

Hold (thanks to conscience) more than half the ball;
O'erthrow this title they have none at all; 26
For never yet might any monarch dare,
Who liv'd to truth, and breath'd a Christian air,
Pretend that Christ, (who came, we all agree,
To bless his people, and to set them free) 30
To make a convert ever one law gave
By which converters made him first a slave.

    Spite of the glosses of a canting priest,
Who talks of charity but means a feast,
Who recommends it (whilst he seems to feel 35
The holy glowings of a real zeal)
To all his hearers, as a deed of worth,
To give them heav'n whom they have robb'd of earth.
Never shall one, one truly honest man,
Who, bless'd with Liberty, reveres her plan, 40
Allow one moment that a savage sire
Could from his wretched race, for childish hire,
By a wild grant, their all, their freedom pass,
And sell his country for a bit of glass.

    Or grant this barb'rous right, let Spain and France,
In slav'ry bred, as purchasers advance; 46
Let them, whilst conscience is at distance hurl'd,
With some gay bawble buy a golden world:
An Englishman, in charter'd freedom born,
Shall spurn the slavish merchandise, shall scorn 50
To take from others, thro' base private views,
What he himself would rather die than lose.

Happy the savage of those early times,
Ere Europe's sons were known and Europe's crimes!
Gold, cursed gold! slept in the womb of earth, 55
Unfelt its mischiefs, as unknown its worth;
In full content he found the truest wealth,
In toil he found diversion, food, and health;
Stranger to ease and luxury of courts,
His sports were labours and his labours sports; 60
His youth was hardy, and his old age green;
Life's morn was vig'rous, and her eve serene;
No rules he held but what were made for use,
No arts he learn'd, nor ills which arts produce;
False lights he follow'd, but believ'd them true; 65
He knew not much, but liv'd to what he knew.

 Happy, thrice happy, now, the savage race,
Since Europe took their gold and gave them grace!
Pastors she sends to help them in their need,
Some who cann't write, with others who cann't read;
And on sure grounds the Gospel pile to rear 71
Sends missionary felons ev'ry year:
Our vices, with more zeal than holy pray'rs,
She teaches them, and in return takes theirs:
Her rank oppressions give them cause to rise, 75
Her want of prudence means and arms supplies,
Whilst her brave rage, not satisfy'd with life,
Rising in blood, adopts the scalping-knife:
Knowledge she gives, enough to make them know
How abject is their state, how deep their woe: 80

The worth of freedom strongly she explains, [chains:
Whilst she bows down and loads their necks with
Faith, too, she plants, for her own ends imprest,
To make them bear the worst and hope the best;
And whilst she teaches, on vile int'rest's plan, 85
As laws of God the wild decrees of man,
Like Pharisees, of whom the Scriptures tell,
She makes them ten times more the sons of Hell.

 But whither do these grave reflections tend?
Are they design'd for any or no end? 90
Briefly but this—to prove that by no act
Which Nature made, that by no equal pact
'Twixt man and man, which might, if Justice heard,
Stand good; that by no benefits conferr'd,
Or purchase made, Europe in chains can hold 95
The sons of India and her mines of gold.
Chance led her there in an accursed hour;
She saw and made the country hers by pow'r;
Nor, drawn by virtue's love from love of fame,
Shall my rash folly controvert the claim, 100
Or wish in thought that title overthrown
Which coincides with and involves my own.

 Europe discover'd India first; I found
My right to Gotham on the selfsame ground;
I first discover'd it, nor shall that plea 105
To her be granted and deny'd to me.
I plead possession, and, till one more bold
Shall drive me out, will that possession hold.

With Europe's rights my kindred rights I twine;
Hers be the Western world, be Gotham mine.   110
   Rejoice, ye happy Gothamites! rejoice;
Lift up your voice on high, a mighty voice,
The voice of gladness; and on ev'ry tongue,
In strains of gratitude, be praises hung,
The praises of so great and good a king;   115
Shall Churchill reign, and shall not Gotham sing?
   As on a day, a high and holy day,
Let ev'ry instrument of musick play,
Ancient and modern; those which drew their birth
(Punctilios laid aside) from Pagan earth,   120
As well as those by Christian made and Jew,
Those known to many, and those known to few;
Those which in whim and frolick lightly flote,
And those which swell the slow and solemn note;
Those which (whilst Reason stands in wonder by)
Make some complexions laugh and others cry;   126
Those which, by some strange faculty of sound,
Can build walls up and raze them to the ground;
Those which can tear up forests by the roots,
And make brutes dance like men, and men like brutes;
Those which, whilst Ridicule leads up the dance,
Make clowns of Monmouth, ape the fops of France;
Those which, where Lady Dulness with Lord May'rs
Presides, disdaining light and trifling airs,
Hallow the feast with psalmody, and those   135
Which, planted in our churches to dispose

And lift the mind to Heaven, are disgrac'd
With what a foppish organist calls Taste:
All, from the fiddle (on which ev'ry fool,
The pert son of dull sire, discharg'd from school,
Serves an apprenticeship in college ease,   141
And rises thro' the gamut to degrees)
To those which (tho' less common, not less sweet)
From fam'd St. Giles's, and more fam'd Vine-street,
(Where Heav'n, the utmost wish of man to grant,
Gave me an old house, and an older aunt)   146
Thornton, whilst Humour pointed out the road
To her arch cub, hath hitch'd into an ode;
All instruments, (attend, ye list'ning Spheres!
Attend, ye sons of men, and hear with ears)   150
All instruments, (nor shall they seek one hand
Impress'd from modern Musick's coxcomb band)
All instruments, self-acted, at my name
Shall pour forth harmony, and loud proclaim,
Loud but yet sweet, to the according globe,   155
My praises, whilst gay Nature, in a robe,
A coxcomb doctor's robe, to the full sound
Keeps time, like Boyce, and the world dances round.

    Rejoice, ye happy Gothamites! rejoice;
Lift up your voice on high, a mighty voice,   160
The voice of gladness; and on ev'ry tongue,
In strains of gratitude, be praises hung,
The praises of so great and good a king;
Shall Churchill reign, and shall not Gotham sing?

Infancy, straining backward from the breast, 165
Tetchy and wayward, what he loveth best
Refusing in his fits, whilst all the while
The mother eyes the wrangler with a smile,
And the fond father sits on t' other side,
Laughs at his moods, and views his spleen with pride,
Shall murmur forth my name, while at his hand 171
Nurse stands interpreter thro' Gotham's land.

 Childhood, who, like an April morn, appears
Sunshine and rain, hopes clouded o'er with fears,
Pleas'd and displeas'd by starts, in passion warm,
In reason weak; who, wrought into a storm, 176
Like to the fretful billows of the deep,
Soon spends his rage, and cries himself asleep;
Who, with a fev'rish appetite oppress'd,
For trifles sighs, but hates them when possess'd,
His trembling lash suspended in the air, 181
Half-bent, and stroking back his long lank hair,
Shall to his mates look up with eager glee,
And let his top go down to prate of me.

 Youth, who, fierce, fickle, insolent and vain,
Impatient urges on to Manhood's reign, 186
Impatient urges on, yet with a cast
Of dear regard looks back on Childhood past,
In the mid-chase, when the hot blood runs high,
And the quick spirits mount into his eye; 190
When pleasure, which he deems his greatest wealth,
Beats in his heart, and paints his cheeks with health;

Volume III.   E

When the chaf'd steed tugs proudly at the rein,
And ere he starts hath run o'er half the plain;
When, wing'd with fear, the stag flies full in view,
And in full cry the eager hounds pursue,   195
Shall shout my praise to hills which shout again,
And ev'n the huntsman stop to cry Amen.

 Manhood, of form erect, who would not bow
Tho' worlds should crack around him; on his brow
Wisdom serene, to passion giving law,   201
Bespeaking love, and yet commanding awe;
Dignity into grace by mildness wrought,
Courage attemper'd, and refin'd by thought;
Virtue supreme enthron'd, within his breast   205
The image of his Maker deep imprest;
Lord of this earth, which trembles at his nod,
With reason bless'd, and only less than God;
Manhood, tho' weeping Beauty kneels for aid,
Tho' Honour calls, in Danger's form array'd,   210
Tho' cloth'd with sackcloth, Justice in the gates,
By wicked elders chain'd, Redemption waits,
Manhood shall steal an hour, a little hour,
(Is 't not a little one?) to hail my pow'r.

 Old Age, a second child, by Nature curst   215
With more and greater evils than the first;
Weak, sickly, full of pains, in ev'ry breath;
Railing at life, and yet afraid of death;
Putting things off, with sage and solemn air,
From day to day, without one day to spare;   220

Without enjoyment covetous of pelf,
Tiresome to friends, and tiresome to himself;
His faculties impair'd, his temper sour'd,
His memory of recent things devour'd
Ev'n with the acting on his shatter'd brain, 225
Tho' the false registers of youth remain;
From morn to ev'ning babbling forth vain praise
Of those rare men who liv'd in those rare days,
When he, the hero of his tale, was young,
Dull repetitions falt'ring on his tongue; 230
Praising gray hairs, sure mark of Wisdom's sway,
Ev'n whilst he curses Time, which made him gray;
Scoffing at youth, ev'n whilst he would afford
All but his gold to have his youth restor'd,
Shall for a moment, from himself set free, 235
Lean on his crutch, and pipe forth praise to me.

 Rejoice, ye happy Gothamites! rejoice;
Lift up your voice on high, a mighty voice,
The voice of gladness; and on ev'ry tongue,
In strains of gratitude, be praises hung, 240
The praises of so great and good a king;
Shall Churchill reign, and shall not Gotham sing?

 Things without life shall in this chorus join,
And dumb to others praise be loud in mine.

 The snow-drop, who, in habit white and plain,
Comes on the herald of fair Flora's train; 246
The coxcomb crocus, flow'r of simple note,
Who by her side struts in a herald's coat;

The tulip, idly glaring to the view,
Who, tho' no clown, his birth from Holland drew,
Who, once full dress'd, fears from his place to stir,
The fop of flow'rs, the More of a parterre ; 252
The woodbine, who her elm in marriage meets,
And brings her dowry in surrounding sweets ;
The lily, silver mistress of the vale, 255
The rose of Sharon, which perfumes the gale ;
The jessamine, with which the queen of flow'rs
To charm her god adorns his fav'rite bow'rs,
Which brides, by the plain hand of Neatness drest,
Unenvy'd rival, wear upon their breast, 260
Sweet as the incense of the morn, and chaste
As the pure zone which circles Dian's waist ;
All flow'rs of various names and various forms,
Which the sun into strength and beauty warms,
From the dwarf daisy, which like infants clings 265
And fears to leave the earth from whence it springs,
To the proud giant of the garden race,
Who, madly rushing to the sun's embrace,
O'ertops her fellows with aspiring aim,
Demands his wedded love, and bears his name ; 270
All, one and all, shall in this chorus join,
And dumb to others praise be loud in mine.

 Rejoice, ye happy Gothamites ! rejoice ;
Lift up your voice on high, a mighty voice,
The voice of gladness ; and on ev'ry tongue, 275
In strains of gratitude, be praises hung,

The praises of so great and good a king;
Shall Churchill reign, and shall not Gotham sing?
   Forming a gloom thro' which, to spleen-struck
Religion horror-stamp'd a passage finds, [minds,
The ivy crawling o'er the hallow'd cell   281
Where some old hermit's wont his beads to tell
By day, by night; the myrtle ever green,
Beneath whose shade Love holds his rites unseen;
The willow, weeping o'er the fatal wave   285
Where many a lover finds a watry grave;
The cypress, sacred held when lovers mourn
Their true love snatch'd away; the laurel, worn
By poets in old time, but destin'd now
In grief to wither on a Whitehead's brow;   290
The fig, which, large as what in India grows,
Itself a grove, gave our first parents clothes;
The vine, which, like a blushing new-made bride,
Clust'ring, empurples all the mountain's side;
The yew, which in the place of sculptur'd stone, 295
Marks out the resting-place of men unknown;
The hedge-row elm, the pine, of mountain race;
The fir, the Scotch fir, never out of place;
The cedar, whose top mates the highest cloud,
Whilst his old father Lebanon grows proud   300
Of such a child, and his vast body, laid
Out many a mile, enjoys the filial shade;
The oak, when living monarch of the wood,
The English oak, which dead commands the flood:

All, one and all, shall in this chorus join, 305
And dumb to others praise be loud in mine.
    Rejoice, ye happy Gothamites! rejoice;
Lift up your voice on high, a mighty voice,
The voice of gladness; and on ev'ry tongue,
In strains of gratitude, be praises hung, 310
The praises of so great and good a king;
Shall Churchill reign, and shall not Gotham sing?
    The show'rs, which make the young hills, like young lambs,
Bound and rebound; the old hills, like old rams,
Unwieldy, jump for joy; the streams which glide,
Whilst Plenty marches smiling by their side, 316
And from their bosom rising Commerce springs;
The winds, which rise with healing on their wings,
Before whose cleansing breath Contagion flies;
The sun, who, travelling in eastern skies, 320
Fresh, full of strength, just risen from his bed,
Tho' in Jove's pastures they were born and bred,
With voice and whip can scarce make his steeds stir,
Step by step, up the perpendicular;
Who, at the hour of eve, panting for rest, 325
Rolls on amain, and gallops down the west
As fast as Jehu, call'd for Ahab's sin,
Drove for a crown, or postboys for an inn;
The moon, who holds o'er night her silver reign,
Regent of tides, and mistress of the brain, 330
Who to her sons, those sons who own her pow'r,
And do her homage at the midnight hour,

Gives madness as a blessing, but dispenses
Wisdom to fools, and damns them with their senses;
The stars, who, by I know not what strange right,
Preside o'er mortals in their own despite, 336
Who, without reason, govern those who most
(How truly judge from thence!) of reason boast,
And by some mighty magic yet unknown
Our actions guide, yet cannot guide their own; 340
All, one and all, shall in this chorus join,
And dumb to others praise be loud in mine.

 Rejoice, ye happy Gothamites! rejoice;
Lift up your voice on high, a mighty voice,
The voice of gladness; and on ev'ry tongue, 345
In strains of gratitude, be praises hung,
The praises of so great and good a king;
Shall Churchill reign, and shall not Gotham sing?

 The moment, minute, hour, day, week, month, year,
Morning and eve, as they in turn appear; 350
Moments and minutes, which, without a crime,
Cann't be omitted in accounts of time,
Or if omitted, (proof we might afford)
Worthy by parliaments to be restor'd; [white,
The Hours, which, dress'd by turns in black and
Ordain'd as handmaids, wait on Day and Night; 356
The Day, those hours I mean when light presides,
And Bus'ness in a cart with Prudence rides;
The Night, those hours I mean with darkness hung,
When Sense speaks free, and Folly holds her tongue;

The morn, when Nature rousing from her strife 361
With death-like sleep, awakes to second life;
The eve, when as unequal to the task
She mercy from her foe descends to ask;
The week, in which six days are kindly given 365
To think of earth, and one to think of heav'n;
The months, twelve sisters, all of diff'rent hue,
Tho' there appears in all a likeness too,
Not such a likeness as, thro' Hayman's works,
Dull Mannerist! in Christians, Jews, and Turks,
Cloys with a sameness in each female face, 371
But a strange something born of Art and Grace,
Which speaks them all, to vary and adorn,
At diff'rent times of the same parents born;
All, one and all, shall in this chorus join, 375
And dumb to others praise be loud in mine.

Rejoice, ye happy Gothamites! rejoice;
Lift up your voice on high, a mighty voice,
The voice of gladness; and on ev'ry tongue,
In strains of gratitude, be praises hung, 380
The praises of so great and good a king;
Shall Churchill reign, and shall not Gotham sing?

Frore January, leader of the year,
Minc'd-pies in van and calves heads in the rear;
Dull February, in whose leaden reign 385
My mother bore a bard without a brain; [cheeks,
March, various, fierce, and wild, with wind-crack'd
By wilder We'shmen led, and crown'd with leeks;

April with fools, and May with bastards blest;
June with White Roses on her rebel breast; 390
July, to whom, the Dog-star in her train,
Saint James gives oysters and Saint Swithin rain;
August, who, banish'd from her Smithfield stand,
To Chelsea flies, with Dogget in her hand;
September, when by custom (right divine) 395
Geese are ordain'd to bleed at Michael's shrine,
Whilst the priest, not so full of grace as wit,
Falls to unbless'd, nor gives the saint a bit;
October, who the cause of freedom join'd,
And gave a second George to bless mankind; 400
November, who at once to grace our earth
Saint Andrew boasts and our Augusta's birth;
December, last of months, but best, who gave
A Christ to man, a Saviour to the slave,
Whilst, falsely grateful, man, at the full feast, 405
To do God honour makes himself a beast;
All, one and all, shall in this chorus join,
And dumb to others praise be loud in mine.

 Rejoice, ye happy Gothamites! rejoice;
Lift up your voice on high, a mighty voice, 410
The voice of gladness; and on ev'ry tongue,
In strains of gratitude, be praises hung,
The praises of so great and good a king;
Shall Churchill reign, and shall not Gotham sing?

 The seasons as they roll; Spring, by her side 415
Lech'ry and Lent, lay-folly and church-pride,

By a rank monk to copulation led,
A tub of sainted salt-fish on her head:
Summer, in light transparent gauze array'd,
Like maids of honour at a masquerade,   420
In bawdry gauze, for which our daughters leave
The fig, more modest, first brought up by Eve,
Panting for breath, inflam'd with lustful fires,
Yet wanting strength to perfect her desires,
Leaning on Sloth, who, fainting with the heat, 425
Stops at each step, and slumbers on his feet:
Autumn, when Nature, who with sorrow feels
Her dread foe Winter treading on her heels,
Makes up in value what she wants in length,
Exerts her pow'rs, and puts forth all her strength,
Bids corn and fruits in full perfection rise,   431
Corn fairly tax'd, and fruits without excise:
Winter, benumb'd with cold, no longer known
By robes of furs, since furs became our own;
A hag, who, loathing all, by all is loath'd,   435
With weekly, daily, hourly, libels cloth'd,
Vile Faction at her heels, who, mighty grown,
Would rule the ruler, and foreclose the throne,
Would turn all state-affairs into a trade,
Make laws one day, the next to be unmade,   440
Beggar at home, a people fear'd abroad,
And, force defeated, make them slaves by fraud;
All, one and all, shall in this chorus join,
And dumb to others praise be loud in mine.

 Rejoice, ye happy Gothamites! rejoice;   445
Lift up your voice on high, a mighty voice,
The voice of gladness; and on ev'ry tongue,
In strains of gratitude, be praises hung,
The praises of so great and good a king;   449
Shall Churchill reign, and shall not Gotham sing?
 The year, grand circle! in whose ample round
The seasons regular and fix'd are bound,
(Who, in his course repeated o'er and o'er,
Sees the same things which he had seen before;
The same stars keep their watch, and the same sun
Runs in the track where he from first hath run; 456
The same moon rules the night; tides ebb and flow,
Man is a puppet, and this world a show;
Their old dull follies old dull fools pursue,
And vice in nothing but in mode is new;   460
He —— a lord (now fair befall that pride,
He liv'd a villain, but a lord he dy'd!)
Dashwood is pious, Berkley fix'd as Fate,
Sandwich (thank Heav'n!), first Minister of State;
And, tho' by fools despis'd, by saints unbless'd,
By friends neglected, and by foes oppress'd,   466
Scorning the servile arts of each court elf,
Founded on honour, Wilkes is still himself;)
The year, encircled with the various train
Which waits and fills the glories of his reign,   470
Shall, taking up this theme, in chorus join,
And dumb to others praise be loud in mine.

  Rejoice, ye happy Gothamites! rejoice;
Lift up your voice on high, a mighty voice,
The voice of gladness; and on ev'ry tongue, 475
In strains of gratitude, be praises hung,
The praises of so great and good a king;
Shall Churchill reign, and shall not Gotham sing?
  Thus far in sport—nor let our critics hence,
Who sell out Monthly trash, and call it Sense, 480
Too lightly of our present labours deem,
Or judge at random of so high a theme:
High is our theme, and worthy are the men
To feel the sharpest stroke of Satire's pen;
But when kind Time a proper season brings, 485
In serious mood to treat of serious things,
Then shall they find, disdaining idle play,
That I can be as grave and dull as they.
  Thus far in sport—nor let half patriots, those
Who shrink from ev'ry blast of Pow'r which blows,
Who, with tame Cowardice familiar grown, 491
Would hear my thoughts, but fear to speak their own;
Who, lest bold truths (to do sage Prudence spite,
Should burst the portals of their lips by night,
Tremble to trust themselves one hour in sleep) 495
Condemn our course, and hold our caution cheap;
When brave Occasion bids, for some great end
When Honour calls the Poet as a friend,
Then shall they find that, ev'n on Danger's brink,
He dares to speak what they scarce dare to think. 500

GOTHAM.

BOOK II.

How much mistaken are the men who think
That all who will without restraint may drink,
May largely drink, ev'n till their bowels burst,
Pleading no right but merely that of thirst,
At the pure waters of the living well　　　　5
Beside whose streams the Muses love to dwell!
Verse is with them a knack, an idle toy,
A rattle gilded o'er, on which a boy
May play untaught, whilst, without art or force,
Make it but jingle, music comes of course.　　10
　Little do such men know the toil, the pains,
The daily, nightly, racking of the brains,
To range the thoughts, the matter to digest,
To cull fit phrases, and reject the rest;
To know the times when Humour on the cheek　15
Of Mirth may hold her sports; when Wit should
And when be silent; when to use the pow'rs [speak,
Of ornament, and how to place the flow'rs,
So that they neither give a tawdry glare,
Nor waste their sweetness in the desert air;　　20
To form (which few can do, and scarcely one,
One critic in an age, can find when done),

To form a plan, to strike a grand outline,
To fill it up, and make the picture shine
A full and perfect piece; to make coy Rhyme   25
Renounce her follies, and with Sense keep time;
To make proud Sense against her nature bend,
And wear the chains of Rhyme, yet call her Friend.

   Some fops there are, among the scribbling tribe,
Who make it all their bus'ness to describe,   30
No matter whether in or out of place;
Studious of finery, and fond of lace,
Alike they trim, as coxcomb Fancy brings,
The rags of beggars and the robes of kings.
Let dull Propriety in state preside   35
O'er her dull children, Nature is their guide,
Wild Nature, who at random breaks the fence
Of those tame drudges Judgment, Taste, and Sense,
Nor would forgive herself the mighty crime
Of keeping terms with Person, Place, and Time. 40

   Let liquid gold emblaze the sun at noon,
With borrow'd beams let silver pale the moon;
Let surges hoarse lash the resounding shore,
Let streams meander, and let torrents roar;
Let them breed up the melancholy breeze   45
To sigh with sighing, sob with sobbing trees;
Let vales embroid'ry wear; let flow'rs be ting'd
With various tints: let clouds be lac'd or fring'd,
They have their wish; like idle monarch boys,
Neglecting things of weight, they sigh for toys; 50

Give them the crown, the sceptre, and the robe,
Who will may take the pow'r and rule the globe.
   Others there are who, in one solemn pace,
With as much zeal as Quakers rail at lace,
Railing at needful ornament, depend   55
On sense to bring them to their journey's end:
They would not (Heav'n forbid!) their course delay,
Nor for a moment step out of the way,
To make the barren road those graces wear   59
Which Nature would, if pleas'd, have planted there.
   Vain men! who blindly thwarting Nature's plan,
Ne'er find a passage to the heart of man;
Who, bred 'mongst fogs in academic land,
Scorn ev'ry thing they do not understand;
Who, destitute of humour, wit, and taste,   65
Let all their little knowledge run to waste,
And frustrate each good purpose, whilst they wear
The robes of Learning with a sloven's air—
Tho' solid reas'ning arms each sterling line,
Tho' Truth declares aloud, "This work is mine," 70
Vice, whilst from page to page dull morals creep,
Throws by the book, and Virtue falls asleep.
   Sense, mere dull, formal, Sense, in this gay Town,
Must have some vehicle to pass her down;
Nor can she for an hour insure her reign,   75
Unless she brings fair Pleasure in her train.
Let her from day to day, from year to year,
In all her grave solemnities appear,

And, with the voice of trumpets, thro' the streets
Deal lectures out to ev'ry one she meets;   80
Half who pass by are deaf, and t' other half
Can hear indeed, but only hear to laugh.

   Quit then, ye graver sons of letter'd Pride!
Taking for once Experience as a guide;
Quit this grand error, this dull college mode;   85
Be your pursuits the same, but change the road;
Write, or at least appear to write, with ease,
And if you mean to profit learn to please.

   In vain for such mistakes they pardon claim,
Because they wield the pen in Virtue's name: 90
Thrice sacred is that name, thrice bless'd the man
Who thinks, speaks, writes, and lives, on such a plan!
This, in himself, himself of course must bless,
But cannot with the world promote success.
He may be strong, but, with effect to speak,   95
Should recollect his readers may be weak:
Plain rigid truths, which saints with comfort bear,
Will make the sinner tremble and despair.
True Virtue acts from love, and the great end
At which she nobly aims is to amend: 100
How then do those mistake who arm her laws
With rigour not their own, and hurt the cause
They mean to help, whilst with a zealot rage
They make that goddess, whom they'd have engage
Our dearest love, in hideous terror rise!   105
Such may be honest, but they cann't be wise.

In her own full and perfect blaze of light
Virtue breaks forth too strong for human sight;
The dazzled eye, that nice but weaker sense,
Shuts herself up in darkness for defence: 110
But to make strong conviction deeper sink,
To make the callous feel, the thoughtless think,
Like God made man, she lays her glory by,
And beams mild comfort on the ravish'd eye:
In earnest most when most she seems in jest, 115
She worms into and winds around the breast;
To conquer vice, of vice appears the friend,
And seems unlike herself to gain her end.
The sons of Sin, to while away the time
Which lingers on their hands, of each black crime
To hush the painful memory, and keep 121
The tyrant Conscience in delusive sleep,
Read on at random, nor suspect the dart
Until they find it rooted in their heart.
'Gainst vice they give their vote, nor know at first 125
That, cursing that, themselves too they have curst;
They see not till they fall into the snares,
Deluded into virtue unawares.
Thus the shrewd doctor, in the spleen-struck mind,
When pregnant Horror sits and broods o'er wind,
Discarding drugs, and striving how to please, 131
Lures on insensibly, by slow degrees,
The patient to those manly sports which bind
The slacken'd sinews, and relieve the mind;

The patient feels a change as wrought by stealth,
And wonders on demand to find it health.　　135
　　Some few, whom Fate ordain'd to deal in rhymes
In other lands, and here in other times,
Whom, waiting at their birth, the midwife Muse
Sprinkled all over with Castalian dews,　　140
To whom true Genius gave his magic pen,
Whom Art by just degrees led up to men;
Some few, extremes well shunn'd, have steer'd be-
These dang'rous rocks, and held the golden mean:　[tween
Sense in their works maintains her proper state,　145
But never sleeps, or labours with her weight:
Grace makes the whole look elegant and gay,
But never dares from sense to run astray:
So nice the master's touch, so great his care,
The colours boldly glow, not idly glare;　　150
Mutually giving and receiving aid,
They set each other off like light and shade,
And, as by stealth, with so much softness blend,
'Tis hard to say where they begin or end:
Both give us charms, and neither gives offence;　155
Sense perfects grace, and grace enlivens sense.
　　Peace to the men who these high honours claim,
Health to their souls, and to their mem'ries fame!
Be it my task, and no mean task, to teach
A rev'rence for that worth I cannot reach:　　160
Let me at distance, with a steady eye,
Observe and mark their passage to the sky;

From envy free, applaud such rising worth,
And praise their heav'n tho' pinion'd down to earth.
 Had I the power I could not have the time, 165
Whilst spirits flow and life is in her prime,
Without a sin 'gainst pleasure, to design
A plan to methodize each thought, each line
Highly to finish, and make ev'ry grace,
In itself charming, take new charms from place. 170
Nothing of books, and little known of men,
When the mad fit comes on I seize the pen;
Rough as they run the rapid thoughts set down,
Rough as they run discharge them on the Town;
Hence rude unfinish'd brats, before their time, 175
Are born into this idle world of Rhyme,
And the poor slattern Muse is brought to bed
With all her imperfections on her head.
Some, as no life appears, no pulses play
Thro' the dull dubious mass, no breath makes way,
Doubt, greatly doubt, till for a glass they call, 181
Whether the child can be bapt z'd at all;
Others on other grounds objections frame,
And, granting that the child may have a name,
Doubt, as the sex might well a midwife pose, 185
Whether they should baptize it Verse or Prose.
 Ev'n what my masters please; bards, mild, meek,
In love to critics stumble now and then. [men,
Something I do myself, and something too,
If they can do it, leave for them to do, 190

In the small compass of my careless page
Critics may find employment for an age;
Without my blunders they were all undone:
I twenty feed where Mason can feed one.
 When Satire stoops, unmindful of her state, 195
To praise the man I love, curse him I hate,
When sense, in tides of passion borne along,
Sinking to prose, degrades the name of song,
The censor smiles, and, whilst my credit bleeds,
With as high relish on the carrion feeds 200
As the proud Earl fed at a turtle feast,
Who, turn'd by gluttony to worse than beast,
Ate till his bowels gush'd upon the floor,
Yet still ate on, and dying call'd for more.
 When loose Digression, like a colt unbroke, 205
Spurning Connexion and her formal yoke,
Bounds thro' the forest, wanders far astray
From the known path, and loves to lose her way,
'Tis a full feast to all the mongrel pack
To run the rambler down and bring her back. 210
 When gay Description, Fancy's fairy child,
Wild without art, and yet with pleasure wild,
Waking with Nature at the morning hour
To the lark's call, walks o'er the op'ning flow'r
Which largely drank all night of heav'n's fresh dew,
And, like a mountain nymph of Dian's crew, 216
So lightly walks she not one mark imprints,
Nor brushes off the dews nor soils the tints;

When thus Description sports, even at the time
That drums should beat and cannons roar in rhyme,
Critics can live on such a fault as that 221
From one month to the other, and grow fat.

 Ye mighty Monthly Judges! in a dearth
Of letter'd blockheads, conscious of the worth
Of my materials, which against your will 225
Oft' you 've confess'd, and shall confess it still;
Materials rich, tho' rude, inflam'd with thought,
Tho' more by fancy than by judgment wrought;
'Take, use them as your own, a work begin,
Which suits your genius well, and weave them in,
Fram'd for the critic loom with critic art, 231
Till thread on thread depending, part on part,
Colour with colour mingling, light with shade,
To your dull taste a formal work is made,
And, having wrought them into one grand piece,
Swear it surpasses Rome and rivals Greece. 236

 Nor think this much—for at one single word,
Soon as the mighty critic fiat's heard,
Science attends their call; their pow'r is own'd,
Order takes place, and Genius is dethron'd! 240
Letters dance into books, defiance hurl'd
At means, as atoms danc'd into a world.

 Me higher bus'ness calls, a greater plan,
Worthy man's whole employ, the good of man,
The good of man committed to my charge; 245
If idle Fancy rambles forth at large,

Careless of such a trust, these harmless lays
May Friendship envy, and may Folly praise,
The crown of Gotham may some Scot assume,
And vagrant Stewarts reign in Churchill's room!

O my poor People! O thou wretched Earth! 251
To whose dear love, tho' not engag'd by birth,
My heart is fix'd, my service deeply sworn,
How, (by thy father can that thought be borne,
For monarchs, would they all but think like me,
Are only fathers in the best degree) 256
How must thy glories fade, in ev'ry land
Thy name be laugh'd to scorn, thy mighty hand
Be shorten'd, and thy zeal, by foes confess'd, 259
Bless'd in thyself, to make thy neighbours bless'd,
Be robb'd of vigour! how must Freedom's pile,
The boast of ages, which adorns the isle,
And makes it great and glorious, fear'd abroad,
Happy at home, secure from force and fraud;
How must that pile, by ancient Wisdom rais'd 265
On a firm rock, by friends admir'd and prais'd,
Envy'd by foes, and wonder'd at by all,
In one short moment into ruins fall,
Should any slip of Stewart's tyrant race,
Or bastard or legitimate, disgrace 270
Thy royal seat of empire! but what care,
What sorrow, must be mine, what deep despair
And self reproaches, should that hated line
Admittance gain thro' any fault of mine!

Curs'd be the cause whence Gotham's evils spring,
Tho' that curs'd cause be found in Gotham's king.
   Let War, with all his needy ruffian band,   277
In pomp of Horror stalk thro' Gotham's land
Knee-deep in blood; let all her stately tow'rs
Sink in the dust; that court which now is ours 280
Become a den, where beasts may, if they can,
A lodging find, nor fear rebuke from man;
Where yellow harvests rise be brambles found;
Where vines now creep let thistles curse the ground;
Dry in her thousand vallys be the rills: 285
Barren the cattle on her thousand hills;
Where Pow'r is plac'd let tigers prowl for prey;
Where Justice lodges let wild asses bray;
Let cormorants in churches make their nest,
And on the sails of commerce bitterns rest; 290
Be all, tho' princes on the earth before,
Her merchants bankrupts, and her marts no more!
Much rather would I, might the will of Fate
Give me to chuse, see Gotham's ruin'd state
By ills on ills, thus to the earth weigh'd down, 295
Than live to see a Stewart wear a crown.
   Let Heav'n in vengeance arm all Nature's host,
Those servants who their Maker know, who boast
Obedience as their glory, and fulfil,
Unquestion'd, their great Master's sacred will; 300
Let raging winds root up the boiling deep,
And with destruction big o'er Gotham sweep;

Let rains rush down, till Faith, with doubtful eye,
Looks for the sign of mercy in the sky;
Let Pestilence in all her horrors rise; 305
Where'er I turn let Famine blast my eyes;
Let the earth yawn, and, ere they 've time to think,
In the deep gulf let all my subjects sink
Before my eyes, whilst on the verge I reel,
Feeling, but as a monarch ought to feel, 310
Not for myself, but them, I 'll kiss the rod,
And, having own'd the justice of my God,
Myself with firmness to the ruin give,
And die with those for whom I wish'd to live!

 This, (but may Heav'n's more merciful decrees
Ne'er tempt his servant with such ills as these) 315
This, or my soul deceives me, I could bear;
But that the Stewart race my crown should wear,
That crown where, highly cherish'd, Freedom shone
Bright as the glories of the mid-day sun; 320
Born and bred slaves, that they, with proud misrule,
Should make brave freeborn men, like boys at school,
To the whip crouch and tremble!—O, that thought!
The lab'ring brain is ev'n to madness brought
By the dread vision; at the mere surmise 325
The thronging spirits as in tumult rise,
My heart, as for a passage, loudly beats,
And turn me where I will distraction meets.

 O my brave Fellows! great in arts and arms,
The wonder of the earth, whom glory warms 330

To high achievements: can your spirits bend,
Thro' base control (ye never can descend
So low by choice) to wear a tyrant's chain,
Or let in Freedom's seat a Stewart reign?
If Fame, who hath for ages, far and wide,   335
Spread in all realms the cowardice, the pride,
The tyranny and falsehood, of those lords,
Contents you not, search England's fair records;
England! where first the breath of life I drew,
Where next to Gotham my best love is due;   340
There once they rul'd, tho' crush'd by William's hand,
They rul'd no more to curse that happy land.

    The first who from his native soil remov'd
Held England's sceptre, a tame tyrant prov'd: 344
Virtue he lack'd, curs'd with those thoughts which
In souls of vulgar stamp to be a king: [spring
Spirit he had not, tho' he laugh'd at laws,
To play the bold-fac'd tyrant with applause;
On practices most mean he rais'd his pride,
And craft oft' gave what wisdom oft' deny'd.   350

    Ne'er could he feel how truly man is blest
In blessing those around him; in his breast,
Crowded with follies, honour found no room:
Mark'd for a coward in his mother's womb,
He was too proud without affronts to live,   355
Too timorous to punish or forgive.

    To gain a crown which had in course of time,
By fair descent, been his, without a crime,

He bore a mother's exile; to secure
A greater crown he basely could endure   360
The spilling of her blood by foreign knife,
Nor dar'd revenge her death who gave him life:
Nay, by fond fear and fond ambition led,
Struck hands with those by whom her blood was shed.

Call'd up to pow'r, scarce warm on England's throne,
He fill'd her court with beggars from his own: 366
Turn where you would the eye with Scots was caught,
Or English knaves, who would be Scotsmen thought.
To vain expence unbounded loose he gave,
The dupe of minions, and of slaves the slave: 370
On false pretences mighty sums he rais'd,
And damn'd those senates rich whom poor he prais'd:
From empire thrown, and doom'd to beg her bread,
On foreign bounty whilst a daughter fed,
He lavish'd sums, for her receiv'd, on men   375
Whose names would fix dishonour on my pen.

Lies were his playthings, parliaments his sport;
Book-worms and catamites engross'd the court:
Vain of the scholar, like all Scotsmen since,
The pedant scholar! he forgot the prince;   380
And having with some trifles stor'd his brain,
Ne'er learn'd or wish'd to learn the arts to reign.
Enough he knew to make him vain and proud,
Mock'd by the wise, the wonder of the crowd;
False friend, false son, false father, and false king,
False wit, false statesman, and false ev'ry thing: 386

When he should act he idly chose to prate,
And pamphlets wrote when he should save the state.
   Religious, if religion holds in whim,
To talk with all he let all talk with him;   390
Not on God's honour, but his own intent,
Not for religion's sake, but argument;
More vain if some sly, artful, High-Dutch slave,
Or, from the Jesuit school, some precious knave
Conviction feign'd, than if, to peace restor'd   395
By his full soldiership, worlds hail'd him Lord.
   Pow'r was his wish, unbounded as his will,
The pow'r without control of doing ill;
But what he wish'd, what he made bishops preach,
And statesmen warrant, hung within his reach,   400
He dar'd not seize: fear gave, to gall his pride,
That freedom to the realm his will deny'd.
   Of treaties fond, o'erweening of his parts,
In ev'ry treaty of his own mean arts
He fell the dupe: peace was his coward care,   405
Ev'n at a time when justice call'd for war.
His pen he 'd draw to prove his lack of wit,
But rather than unsheath the sword submit.
Truth fairly must record; and, pleas'd to live
In league with mercy, justice may forgive   410
Kingdoms betray'd, and worlds resign'd to Spain,
But never can forgive a Raleigh slain.
   At length (with white let Freedom mark that year),
Not fear'd by those whom most he wish'd to fear,

Not lov'd by those whom most he wish'd to love, 415
He went to answer for his faults above,
To answer to that God from whom alone
He claim'd to hold and to abuse the throne,
Leaving behind a curse to all his line,
The bloody legacy of Right Divine. 420

With many virtues which a radiance fling
Round private men, with few which grace a king,
And speak the monarch, at the time of life
When passion holds with reason doubtful strife,
Succeeded Charles, by a mean sire undone, 425
Who envy'd virtue even in a son.

His youth was froward, turbulent, and wild;
He took the man up ere he left the child;
His soul was eager for imperial sway
Ere he had learn'd the lesson to obey. 430
Surrounded by a fawning flatt'ring throng,
Judgment each day grew weak, and humour strong;
Wisdom was treated as a noisome weed,
And all his follies let to run to seed.

What ills from such beginnings needs must spring!
What ills to such a land from such a king! 436
What could she hope! what had she not to fear!
Base Buckingham possess'd his youthful ear;
Strafford and Laud, when mounted on the throne,
Engross'd his love, and made him all their own; 440
Strafford and Laud, who boldly dar'd avow
The trait'rous doctrines taught by Tories now;

Each strove t' undo him in his turn and hour,
The first with pleasure, and the last with pow'r.
  Thinking (vain thought, disgraceful to the throne!)
That all mankind were made for kings alone, 446
That subjects were but slaves, and what was whim,
Or worse, in common men, was law in him;
Drunk with Prerogative, which Fate decreed
To guard good kings, and tyrants to mislead; 450
Which in a fair proportion to deny
Allegiance dares not, which to hold too high
No good can wish no coward king can dare,
And held too high no English subject bear:
Besieg'd by men of deep and subtle arts, 455
Men void of principle, and damn'd with parts,
Who saw his weakness, made their king their tool,
Then most a slave when most he seem'd to rule:
Taking all public steps for private ends,
Deceiv'd by fav'rites, whom he called friends, 460
He had not strength enough of soul to find
That monarchs, meant as blessings to mankind,
Sink their great state, and stamp their fame undone,
When what was meant for all they give to one.
List'ning uxorious whilst a woman's prate 465
Modell'd the church and parcell'd out the state,
Whilst (in the state not more than women read)
High-churchmen preach'd, and turn'd his pious head;
Tutor'd to see with ministerial eyes,
Forbid to hear a loyal nation's cries; 470

G iij

Made to believe (what cann't a fav'rite do?)
He heard a nation hearing one or two;
Taught by state-quacks himself secure to think,
And out of danger ev'n on danger's brink;
Whilst pow'r was daily crumbling from his hand,
Whilst murmurs ran thro' an insulted land,   476
As if to sanction tyrants Heav'n was bound,
He proudly sought the ruin which he found.

    Twelve years, twelve tedious and inglorious years,
Did England, crush'd by pow'r and aw'd by fears, 480
Whilst proud Oppression struck at Freedom's root,
Lament her senates lost, her Hampden mute:
Illegal taxes and oppressive loans,
In spite of all her pride, call'd forth her groans:
Patience was heard her griefs aloud to tell,   485
And Loyalty was tempted to rebel.

    Each day new acts of outrage shook the state,
New courts were rais'd to give new doctrines weight;
State-Inquisitions kept the realm in awe,
And curs'd Star-Chambers made or rul'd the law;
Juries were pack'd, and judges were unsound;   490
Thro' the whole kingdom not one Pratt was found.

    From the first moments of his giddy youth
He hated senates, for they told him truth:
At length against his will compell'd to treat,   495
Those whom he could not fright he strove to cheat,
With base dissembling every grievance heard,
And often giving often broke his word.

O! where shall helpless Truth for refuge fly,
If kings who should protect her dare to lie? 500
 Those who, the gen'ral good their real aim,
Sought in their country's good their monarch's fame;
Those who were anxious for his safety; those
Who were induc'd by duty to oppose,
Their truth suspected, and their worth unknown,
He held as foes and traitors to his throne, 506
Nor found his fatal error till the hour
Of saving him was gone and past; till pow'r
Had shifted hands, to blast his hapless reign,
Making their faith and his repentance vain. 510
 Hence (be that curse confin'd to Gotham's foes)
War, dread to mention, Civil War, arose;
All acts of outrage and all acts of shame
Stalk'd forth at large, disguis'd with Honour's name:
Rebellion, raising high her bloody hand, 515
Spread universal havoc thro' the land:
With zeal for party, and with passion drunk,
In public rage all private love was sunk;
Friend against friend, brother 'gainst brother stood,
And the son's weapon drank the father's blood: 520
Nature, aghast, and fearful lest her reign
Should last no longer, bled in ev'ry vein.
 Unhappy Stewart! harshly tho' that name
Grates on my ear, I should have dy'd with shame
To see my king before his subjects stand, 525
And at their bar hold up his royal hand;

At their commands to hear the monarch plead,
By their decrees to see that monarch bleed!
What tho' thy faults were many and were great?
What tho' they shook the basis of the state? 530
In royalty secure thy person stood,
And sacred was the fountain of thy blood.
Vile ministers, who dar'd abuse their trust, 533
Who dar'd seduce a king to be unjust,
Vengeance, with justice leagu'd, with pow'r made [strong,
Had nobly crush'd. "The king could do no wrong."

Yet grieve not, Charles! nor thy hard fortunes blame;
They took thy life, but they secur'd thy fame.
Their greater crimes made thine like specks appear,
From which the sun in glory is not clear. 540
Hadst thou in peace and years resign'd thy breath,
At Nature's call hadst thou laid down in death,
As in a sleep, thy name, by Justice borne
On the four winds, had been in pieces torn.
Pity, the virtue of a gen'rous soul, 545
Sometimes the vice, hath made thy mem'ry whole.
Misfortunes gave what virtue could not give,
And bade, the tyrant slain, the Martyr live.

Ye Princes of the earth! ye mighty few!
Who worlds subduing cann't yourselves subdue,
Who, goodness scorn'd, wish only to be great, 551
Whose breath is blasting, and whose voice is fate,
Who own no law, no reason, but your will,
And scorn restraint, tho' 't is from doing ill,

Who of all passions groan beneath the worst, 555
Then only bless'd when they make others curst;
Think not for wrongs like these unscourg'd to live;
Long may ye sin, and long may Heav'n forgive;
But when ye least expect, in sorrow's day,
Vengeance shall fall more heavy for delay; 560
Nor think that vengeance heap'd on you alone
Shall (poor amends) for injur'd worlds atone;
No; like some base distemper, which remains
Transmitted from the tainted father's veins
In the son's blood, such broad and gen'ral crimes 565
Shall call down vengeance ev'n to latest times,
Call vengeance down on all who bear your name,
And make their portion bitterness and shame.

 From land to land for years compell'd to roam,
Whilst Usurpation lorded it at home, 570
Of majesty unmindful, forc'd to fly,
Not daring, like a king, to reign or die,
Recall'd to repossess his lawful throne,
More at his people's seeking than his own,
Another Charles succeeded. In the school 575
Of travel he had learn'd to play the fool,
And, like pert pupils with dull tutors sent
To shame their country on the continent,
From love of England by long absence wean'd,
From ev'ry court he ev'ry folly glean'd, 580
And was, so close do evil habits cling,
Till crown'd a beggar, and when crown'd no king.

Those grand and gen'ral pow'rs which Heav'n design'd
An instance of his mercy to mankind,
Were lost, in storms of dissipation hurl'd,   585
Nor would he give one hour to bless a world:
Lighter than levity which strides the blast,
And of the present fond forgets the past,
He chang'd and chang'd, but, ev'ry hope to curse,
Chang'd only from one folly to a worse: 590
State he resign'd to those whom state could please;
Careless of majesty, his wish was ease;
Pleasure, and pleasure only, was his aim;
Kings of less wit might hunt the bubble fame:
Dignity thro' his reign was made a sport,   595
Nor dar'd Decorum show her face at court:
Morality was held a standing jest,
And faith a necessary fraud at best:
Courtiers, their monarch ever in their view,
Possess'd great talents, and abus'd them too: 600
Whate'er was light, impertinent, and vain,
Whate'er was loose, indecent, and profane,
(So ripe was folly folly to acquit)
Stood all absolv'd in that poor bawble wit.

In gratitude, alas! but little read,   605
He let his father's servants beg their bread,
His father's faithful servants and his own,
To place the foes of both around his throne.

Bad counsels he embrac'd thro' indolence,
'Thro' love of ease, and not thro' want of sense: 610

He saw them wrong, but rather let them go
As right, than take the pains to make them so.
 Women rul'd all, and ministers of state
Were for commands at toilettes forc'd to wait;
Women, who have as monarchs grac'd the land, 615
But never govern'd well at second-hand.
 To make all other errors slight appear,
In mem'ry fix'd stand Dunkirk and Tangier;
In mem'ry fix'd so deep, that time in vain
Shall strive to wipe those records from the brain. 620
Amboyna stands—Gods! that a king should hold
In such high estimate vile paltry gold,
And of his duty be so careless found,
That when the blood of subjects from the ground
For vengeance call'd, he should reject their cry. 625
And, brib'd from honour, lay his thunders by,
Give Holland peace, whilst English victims groan'd,
And butcher'd subjects wander'd unaton'd!
O! dear, deep injury to England's fame,
To them, to us, to all! to him deep shame! 630
Of all the passions which from frailty spring,
Av'rice is that which least becomes a king.
 To crown the whole, scorning the public good,
Which thro' his reign he little understood
Or little heeded, with too narrow aim 635
He reassum'd a bigot brother's claim,
And having made time-serving senates bow,
Suddenly dy'd, that brother best knew how.

No matter how—he slept amongst the dead,
And James his brother reigned in his stead : 640
But such a reign—so glaring an offence
In ev'ry step 'gainst freedom, law, and sense,
'Gainst all the rights of Nature's gen'ral plan,
'Gainst all which constitutes an Englishman,
That the relation would mere fiction seem, 645
The mock creation of a poet's dream,
And the poor bards would, in this sceptic age,
Appear as false as their historian's page.

Ambitious folly seiz'd the seat of wit,
Christians were forc'd by bigots to submit; 650
Pride without sense, without religion zeal,
Made daring inroads on the commonweal;
Stern Persecution rais'd her iron rod,
And call'd the pride of kings the pow'r of God;
Conscience and fame were sacrific'd to Rome, 655
And England wept at Freedom's sacred tomb.

Her laws despis'd, her constitution wrench'd
From its due nat'ral frame, her rights retrench'd
Beyond a coward's suff'rance, conscience forc'd,
And healing justice from the crown divorc'd, 660
Each moment pregnant with vile acts of pow'r,
Her patriot bishops sentenc'd to the Tow'r,
Her Oxford (who yet loves the Stewart name)
Branded with arbitrary marks of shame, 664
She wept—but wept not long; to arms she flew,
At Honour's call th' avenging sword she drew,

Turn'd all her terrors on the tyrant's head,
And sent him in despair to beg his bread;
Whilst she, (may ev'ry state in such distress
Dare with such zeal, and meet with such success) 670
Whilst she, (may Gotham, should my abject mind
Choose to enslave rather than free mankind,
Pursue her steps, tear the proud tyrant down,
Nor let me wear if I abuse the crown)
Whilst she, (thro' ev'ry age, in ev'ry land, 675
Written in gold, let Revolution stand)
Whilst she, secur'd in liberty and law,
Found what she sought, a saviour in Nassau. 678

GOTHAM.

BOOK III.

Can the fond mother from herself depart?
Can she forget the darling of her heart,
The little darling whom she bore and bred,
Nurs'd on her knees, and at her bosom fed,
To whom she seem'd her ev'ry thought to give, 5
And in whose life alone she seem'd to live?
Yes, from herself the mother may depart,
She may forget the darling of her heart,
The little darling whom she bore and bred,
Nurs'd on her knees, and at her bosom fed, 10
To whom she seem'd her ev'ry thought to give,
And in whose life alone she seem'd to live;
But I cannot forget, whilst life remains,
And pours her current thro' these swelling veins,
Whilst Mem'ry offers up at Reason's shrine, 15
But I cannot forget that Gotham's mine.

  Can the stern mother, than the brutes more wild,
From her disnatur'd breast tear her young child,
Flesh of her flesh, and of her bone the bone,
And dash the smiling babe against a stone? 20
Yes, the stern mother, than the brutes more wild,
From her disnatur'd breast may tear her child,
Flesh of her flesh, and of her bone the bone,
And dash the smiling babe against a stone;

But I, (forbid it, Heav'n!) but I can ne'er 25
The love of Gotham from this bosom tear,
Can ne'er so far true royalty pervert
From its fair course to do my people hurt.

 With how much ease, with how much confidence,
As if, superior to each grosser sense 30
Reason had only, in full pow'r array'd,
To manifest her will, and be obey'd,
Men make resolves, and pass into decrees
The motions of the mind! with how much ease,
In such resolves, doth passion make a flaw, 35
And bring to nothing what was rais'd to law!

 In empire young, scarce warm on Gotham's throne,
The dangers and the sweets of pow'r unknown,
Pleas'd, tho' I scarce know why, like some young child
Whose little senses each new toy turns wild, 40
How do I hold sweet dalliance with my crown,
And wanton with dominion! how lay down,
Without the sanction of a precedent,
Rules of most large and absolute extent,
Rules which from sense of public virtue spring, 45
And all at once commence a patriot king!

 But, for the day of trial is at hand,
And the whole fortunes of a mighty land
Are stak'd on me, and all their weal or wo
Must from my good or evil conduct flow, 50
Will I, or can I, on a fair review,
As I assume that name deserve it too?

       H ij

Have I well weigh'd the great the noble part
I'm now to play? have I explor'd my heart,
That labyrinth of fraud, that deep dark cell, 55
Where, unsuspected ev'n by me, may dwell
Ten thousand follies? have I found out there
What I am fit to do and what to bear?
Have I trac'd ev'ry passion to its rise,
Nor spar'd one lurking seed of treach'rous vice? 60
Have I familiar with my nature grown?
And am I fairly to myself made known?

A patriot king—Why, 'tis a name which bears
The more immediate stamp of Heav'n, which wears
The nearest, best, resemblance we can show 65
Of God above thro' all his works below.

To still the voice of discord in the land,
To make weak Faction's discontented band,
Detected, weak, and crumbling to decay,
With hunger pinch'd on their own vitals prey; 70
Like brethren in the self-same int'rests warm'd,
Like diff'rent bodies with one soul inform'd;
To make a nation nobly rais'd above
All meaner thought grow up in common love;
To give the laws due vigour, and to hold 75
That secret balance temperate yet bold,
With such an equal hand, that those who fear
May yet approve, and own my justice clear;
To be a common father, to secure
The weak from violence, from pride the poor; 80

Vice and her sons to banish in disgrace,
To make Corruption dread to show her face;
To bid afflicted Virtue take new state,
And be at last acquainted with the great;
Of all religions to elect the best, 85
Nor let her priests be made a standing jest;
Rewards for worth with lib'ral hand to carve,
To love the arts, nor let the artists starve;
To make fair plenty thro' the realm increase,
Give fame in war, and happiness in peace; 90
To see my people, virt'ous, great, and free,
And know that all those blessings flow from me;
O! 'tis a joy too exquisite, a thought,
Which flatters Nature more than flatt'ry ought;
'Tis a great, glorious, task, for man too hard, 95
But not less great, less glorious, the reward;
The best reward which here to man is giv'n,
'Tis more than earth, and little short of heav'n:
A task (if such comparison may be)
The same in nature, diff'ring in degree, 100
Like that which God, on whom for aid I call,
Performs with ease, and yet performs to all.

How much do they mistake, how little know
Of kings, of kingdoms, and the pains which flow
From royalty, who fancy that a crown, 105
Because it glistens, must be lin'd with down!
With outside show and vain appearance caught,
They look no farther, and, by Folly taught,

Prize high the toys of thrones, but never find
One of the many cares which lurk behind.   110
The gem they worship which a crown adorns,
Nor once suspect that crown is lin'd with thorns.
O might Reflection Folly's place supply!
Would we one moment use her piercing eye,   114
Then should we know what wo from grandeur
And learn to pity not to envy kings.   [springs,

  The villager, born humbly and bred hard,
Content his wealth, and Poverty his guard,
In action simply just, in conscience clear,
By guilt untainted, undisturb'd by fear,   120
His means but scanty, and his wants but few,
Labour his bus'ness, and his pleasure too,
Enjoys more comforts in a single hour
Than ages give the wretch condemn'd to pow'r.

  Call'd up by health he rises with the day,   125
And goes to work as if he went to play,
Whistling off toils, one half of which might make
The stoutest Atlas of a palace quake;
'Gainst heat and cold, which make us cowards faint,
Harden'd by constant use, without complaint   130
He bears what we should think it death to bear:
Short are his meals and homely is his fare;
His thirst he slakes at some pure neighb'ring brook,
Nor asks for sauce where Appetite stands cook.
When the dews fall, and when the sun retires   135
Behind the mountains, when the village fires,

Which, waken'd all at once, speak supper nigh,
At distance catch, and fix his longing eye,
Homeward he hies, and with his manly brood
Of raw-bon'd cubs enjoys that clean coarse food 140
Which, season'd with good humour, his fond bride
'Gainst his return is happy to provide;
Then, free from care, and free from thought, he creeps
Into his straw, and till the morning sleeps.

   Not so the king—with anxious cares opprest 145
His bosom labours, and admits not rest:
A glorious wretch! he sweats beneath the weight
Of majesty, and gives up ease for state:
Ev'n when his smiles, which by the fools of pride
Are treasur'd and preserv'd from side to side, 150
Fly round the court, ev'n when compell'd by form
He seems most calm, his soul is in a storm!
Care, like a spectre, seen by him alone,
With all her nest of vipers, round his throne
By day crawls full in view; when night bids sleep,
Sweet nurse of Nature! o'er the senses creep, 156
When Misery herself no more complains,
And slaves, if possible, forget their chains,
Tho' his sense weakens, tho' his eyes grow dim,
That rest which comes to all comes not to him. 160
Ev'n at that hour Care, tyrant Care! forbids
The dew of sleep to fall upon his lids;
From night to night she watches at his bed,
Now as one mop'd sits brooding o'er his head,

Anon she starts, and, borne on ravens wings, 165
Croaks forth aloud—Sleep was not made for kings.

   Thrice hath the moon, who governs this vast ball,
Who rules most absolute o'er me and all,
To whom by full conviction taught to bow,
At new, at full, I pay the duteous vow; 170
Thrice hath the moon her wonted course pursu'd,
Thrice hath she lost her form, and thrice renew'd,
Since, (bless'd be that season, for before
I was a mere mere mortal, and no more,
One of the herd, a lump of common clay, 175
Inform'd with life, to die and pass away)
Since I became a king, and Gotham's throne
With full and ample pow'r became my own;
Thrice hath the moon her wonted course pursu'd,
Thrice hath she lost her form, and thrice renew'd, 180
Since sleep, kind sleep! who like a friend supplies
New vigour for new toil, hath clos'd these eyes:
Nor, if my toils are answer'd with success,
And I am made an instrument to bless
The people whom I love, shall I repine; 185
Theirs be the benefit, the labour mine.

   Mindful of that high rank in which I stand,
Of millions lord, sole ruler in the land,
Let me, and Reason shall her aid afford,
Rule my own spirit, of myself be lord. 190
With an ill grace that monarch wears his crown
Who, stern and hard of nature, wears a frown

'Gainst faults in other men, yet all the while
Meets his own vices with a partial smile.
How can a king (yet on record we find   195
Such kings have been, such curses of mankind)
Enforce that law 'gainst some poor subject elf
Which Conscience tells him he hath broke himself?
Can he some petty rogue to justice call
For robbing one, when he himself robs all?   200
Must not, unless extinguish'd, conscience fly
Into his cheek, and blast his fading eye,
To scourge th' oppressor, when the state, distress'd
And sunk to ruin, is by him oppress'd?
Against himself doth he not sentence give?   205
If one must die t' other's not fit to live.

  Weak is that throne, and in itself unsound,
Which takes not solid virtue for its ground.
All envy pow'r in others, and complain
Of that which they would perish to obtain.   210
Nor can those spirits, turbulent and bold,
Not to be aw'd by threats nor bought with gold,
Be hush'd to peace, but when fair legal sway
Makes it their real int'rest to obey,
When kings, and none but fools can then rebel, 215
Not less in virtue than in pow'r excel.

  Be that my object, that my constant care,
And may my soul's best wishes centre there;
Be it my task to seek, nor seek in vain,
Not only how to live but how to reign,   220

And to those virtues which from reason spring,
And grace the man, join those which grace the king.
 First, (for strict duty bids my care extend
And reach to all who on that care depend,
Bids me with servants keep a steady hand, 225
And watch o'er all my proxies in the land)
First, (and that method reason shall support)
Before I look into and purge my court,
Before I cleanse the stable of the state,
Let me fix things which to myself relate: 230
That done, and all accounts well settled here,
In resolution firm, in honour clear,
Tremble, ye Slaves! who dare abuse your trust,
Who dare be villains when your king is just.
 Are there, amongst those officers of state 235
To whom our sacred pow'r we delegate,
Who hold our place and office in the realm,
Who, in our name commission'd, guide the helm;
Are there who, trusting to our love of ease,
Oppress our subjects, wrest our just decrees, 240
And make the laws, warp'd from their fair intent,
To speak a language which they never meant;
Are there such men, and can the fools depend
On holding out in safety to their end?
Can they so much, from thoughts of danger free, 245
Deceive themselves, so much misdeem of me,
To think that I will prove a statesman's tool,
And live a stranger where I ought to rule?

What! to myself and to my state unjust,
Shall I from ministers take things on trust, 250
And, sinking low the credit of my throne,
Depend upon dependents of my own?
Shall I, most certain source of future cares,
Not use my judgment, but depend on theirs?
Shall I, true puppet-like, be mock'd with state, 255
Have nothing but the name of being great,
Attend at counsels which I must not weigh,
Do what they bid, and what they dictate say,
Enrob'd, and hoisted up into my chair,
Only to be a royal cipher there? 260
Perish the thought—'t is treason to my throne—
And who but thinks it, could his thoughts be known,
Insults me more than he who, leagu'd with Hell,
Shall rise in arms, and 'gainst my crown rebel.

    The wicked statesman, whose false heart pursues
A train of guilt, who acts with double views, 266
And wears a double face; whose base designs
Strike at his monarch's throne; who undermines
Ev'n whilst he seems his wishes to support;
Who seizes all departments; packs a court; 270
Maintains an agent on the judgment-seat
To screen his crimes, and make his frauds complete;
New models armies, and around the throne
Will suffer none but creatures of his own;
Conscious of such his baseness, well may try, 275
Against the light to shut his master's eye,

To keep him coop'd, and far remov'd from those
Who, brave and honest, dare his crimes disclose,
Nor ever let him in one place appear
Where truth, unwelcome truth, may wound his ear.
    Attempts like these, well weigh'd, themselves proclaim,   281
And whilst they publish baulk their author's aim.
Kings must be blind into such snares to run,
Or, worse, with open eyes must be undone.
The minister of honesty and worth   285
Demands the day to bring his actions forth,
Calls on the sun to shine with fiercer rays,
And braves that trial which must end in praise.
None fly the day and seek the shades of night
But those whose actions cannot bear the light;   290
None wish their king in ignorance to hold
But those who feel that knowledge must unfold
Their hidden guilt; and, that dark mist dispell'd
By which their places and their lives are held,
Confusion wait them, and, by Justice led,   295
In vengeance fall on ev'ry traitor's head!
    Aware of this, and caution'd 'gainst the pit
Where kings have oft' been lost, shall I submit,
And rust in chains like these? shall I give way,
And, whilst my helpless subjects fall a prey   300
To pow'r abus'd, in ignorance sit down,
Nor dare assert the honour of my crown?
When Stern Rebellion, (if that odious name
Justly belongs to those whose only aim

Is to preserve their country; who oppose, 305
In honour leagu'd, none but their country's foes;
Who only seek their own, and found their cause
In due regard for violated laws)
When stern Rebellion, who no longer feels
Nor fears rebuke, a nation at her heels, 310
A nation up in arms, tho' strong not proud,
Knocks at the palace-gate, and, calling loud
For due redress, presents, from Truth's fair pen,
A list of wrongs not to be borne by men;
How must that king be humbled, how disgrace 315
All that is royal in his name and place,
Who, thus call'd forth to answer, can advance
No other plea but that of ignorance!
A vile defence, which, was his all at stake,
The meanest subject well might blush to make; 320
A filthy source, from whence shame ever springs;
A stain to all, but most a stain to kings.
The soul, with great and manly feelings warm'd,
Panting for knowledge, rests not till inform'd;
And shall not I, fir'd with the glorious zeal, 325
Feel those brave passions which my subjects feel?
Or can a just excuse from ign'rance flow
To me, whose first great duty is—to know?

   Hence, Ignorance!—thy settled, dull, blank eye
Would hurt me tho' I knew no reason why— 330
Hence, Ignorance!—thy slavish shackles bind
The free-born soul, and lethargy the mind—

Of thee, begot by Pride, who look'd with scorn
On ev'ry meaner match, of thee was born
That grave inflexibility of soul 335
Which Reason cann't convince nor fear control,
Which neither arguments nor pray'rs can reach,
And nothing less than utter ruin teach—
Hence, Ignorance!—hence to that depth of night
Where thou wast born, where not one gleam of light
May wound thine eye—hence to some dreary cell 341
Where monks with superstition love to dwell,
Or in some college sooth thy lazy pride,
And with the heads of colleges reside;
Fit mate for Royalty thou canst not be, 345
And if no mate for kings no mate for me.

   Come, Study! like a torrent swell'd with rains,
Which rushing down the mountains o'er the plains
Spreads horror wide, and yet, in horror kind,
Leaves seeds of future fruitfulness behind: 350
Come, Study!—painful tho' thy course, and slow,
Thy real worth by thy effects we know—
Parent of Knowledge, come—not thee I call
Who, grave and dull, in college or in hall
Dost sit, all solemn sad, and, moping, weigh 355
Things which, when found, thy labours cann't repay--
Nor in one hand, fit emblem of thy trade,
A rod; in t' other, gaudily array'd,
A hornbook gilt and letter'd, call I thee,
Who dost in form preside o'er A, B, C— 360

Nor (Siren tho' thou art, and thy strange charms,
As 't were by magic, lure men to thy arms)
Do I call thee who, thro' a winding maze,
A labyrinth of puzzling pleasing ways,
Dost lead us at the last to those rich plains 365
Where in full glory real Science reigns;
Fair tho' thou art, and lovely to mine eye,
Tho' full rewards in thy possession lie
To crown man's wish, and do thy fav'rites grace,
Tho' (was I station'd in an humbler place) 370
I could be ever happy in thy sight,
Toil with thee all the day, and thro' the night
Toil on from watch to watch, bidding my eye,
Fast rivetted on science, sleep defy,
Yet (such the hardships which from empire flow) 375
Must I thy sweet society forego,
And to some happy rival's arms resign
Those charms which can, alas! no more be mine.

 No more from hour to hour, from day to day,
Shall I pursue thy steps, and urge my way 380
Where eager love of science calls; no more
Attempt those paths which man ne'er trod before;
No more the mountain scal'd, the desert crost,
Losing myself, nor knowing I was lost,
Travel thro' woods, thro' wilds, from morn to night,
From night to morn, yet travel with delight, 386
And having found thee lay me down content,
Own all my toil well paid, my time well spent.

Farewell, ye Muses! too—for such mean things
Must not presume to dwell with mighty kings— 390
Farewell, ye Muses!—tho' it cuts my heart,
Ev'n to the quick, we must for ever part.

 When the fresh morn bade lusty Nature wake;
When the birds sweetly twitt'ring thro' the brake
Tun'd their soft pipes; when from the neighb'ring bloom
Sipping the dew, each zephyr stole perfume;
When all things with new vigour were inspir'd, 397
And seem'd to say they never could be tir'd,
How often have we stray'd, whilst sportive Rhyme
Deceiv'd the way, and clipp'd the wings of Time,
O'er hill, o'er dale! how often laugh'd to see 401
Yourselves made visible to none but me!
The clown, his work suspended, gape and stare,
And seem'd to think that I convers'd with air!

 When the sun, beating on the parched soil, 405
Seem'd to proclaim an interval of toil;
When a faint languor crept thro' ev'ry breast,
And things most us'd to labour wish'd for rest,
How often, underneath a rev'rend oak,
Where safe, and fearless of the impious stroke, 410
Some sacred Dryad liv'd; or in some grove
Where, with capricious fingers, Fancy wove
Her fairy bow'r, whilst Nature all the while
Look'd on, and view'd her mock'ries with a smile,
Have we held converse sweet! how often laid, 415
Fast by the Thames, in Ham's inspiring shade,

Amongst those poets which make up your train,
And after death pour forth the sacred strain,
Have I, at your command, in verse grown gray,
But not impair'd, heard Dryden tune that lay   420
Which might have drawn an angel from his sphere,
And kept him from his office list'ning here!

   When dreary Night, with Morpheus in her train,
Led on by Silence to resume her reign,
With darkness covering, as with a robe,   425
This scene of levity, blank'd half the globe,
How oft', enchanted with your heav'nly strains,
Which stole me from myself, which in soft chains
Of music bound my soul, how oft' have I,
Sounds more than human floating thro' the sky,   430
Attentive sat, whilst Night, against her will,
Transported with the harmony, stood still!
How oft' in raptures, which man scarce could bear,
Have I, when gone, still thought the Muses there,
Still heard their music, and, as mute as death,   435
Sat all attention, drew in ev'ry breath,
Lest, breathing all too rudely, I should wound
And mar that magic excellence of sound,
Then, sense returning with return of day,
Have chid the night which fled so fast away!   440

   Such my pursuits, and such my joys of yore,
Such were my mates, but now my mates no more.
Plac'd out of Envy's walk (for Envy sure
Would never haunt the cottage of the poor,

Would never stoop to wound my homespun lays) 445
With some few friends, and some small share of praise,
Beneath oppression, undisturb'd by strife,
In peace I trod the humble vale of life.
Farewell these scenes of ease, this tranquil state;
Welcome the troubles which on empire wait: 450
Light toys from this day forth I disavow;
They pleas'd me once, but cannot suit me now:
To common men all common things are free,
What honours them might fix disgrace on me.
Call'd to a throne, and o'er a mighty land 455
Ordain'd to rule, my head, my heart, my hand,
Are all engross'd; each private view withstood,
And task'd to labour for the public good:
Be this my study; to this one great end
May ev'ry thought, may ev'ry action tend! 460

 Let me the page of history turn o'er,
Th' instructive page, and heedfully explore
What faithful pens of former times have wrote
Of former kings; what they did worthy note,
What worthy blame; and from the sacred tomb 465
Where righteous monarchs sleep, where laurels bloom
Unhurt by time, let me a garland twine
Which robbing not their fame may add to mine.
 Nor let me with a vain and idle eye
Glance o'er those scenes, and in a hurry fly 470
Quick as a post which travels day and night;
Nor let me dwell there, lur'd by false delight,

And, into barren theory betray'd,
Forget that monarchs are for action made.
When am'rous Spring, repairing all his charms, 475
Calls Nature forth from hoary Winter's arms,
Where, like a virgin to some lecher sold,
Three wretched months she lay benumb'd and cold;
When the weak flow'r, which shrinking from the
Of the rude north, and timorous of death,   [breath
To its kind mother Earth for shelter fled,   481
And on her bosom hid its tender head,
Peeps forth afresh, and, cheer'd by milder skies,
Bids in full splendor all her beauties rise,
The hive is up in arms—expert to teach, 485
Nor, proudly, to be taught unwilling, each
Seems from her fellow a new zeal to catch;
Strength in her limbs, and on her wings dispatch,
The bee goes forth; from herb to herb she flies, 489
From flow'r to flow'r, and loads her lab'ring thighs
With treasur'd sweets, robbing those flow'rs which,
Find not themselves made poorer by the theft, [left,
Their scents as lively, and their looks as fair,
As if the pillager had not been there.
Ne'er doth she flit on pleasure's silken wing; 495
Ne'er doth she, loit'ring, let the bloom of Spring
Unrifled pass, and on the downy breast
Of some fair flow'r indulge untimely rest:
Ne'er doth she, drinking deep of those rich dews
Which chymist Night prepar'd, that faith abuse 500

Due to the hive, and, selfish in her toils,
To her own private use convert the spoils:
Love of the stock first call'd her forth to roam,
And to the stock she brings her booty home.
　Be this my pattern—As becomes a king, 　505
Let me fly all abroad on Reason's wing:
Let mine eye, like the lightning, thro' the earth
Run to and fro, nor let one deed of worth,
In any place and time, nor let one man,
Whose actions may enrich dominion's plan, 　510
Escape my note: be all, from the first day
Of Nature to this hour, be all my prey.
From those whom Time, at the desire of Fame,
Hath spar'd, let Virtue catch an equal flame:
From those who, not in mercy, but in rage, 　515
Time hath repriev'd to damn from age to age,
Let me take warning, lesson'd to distil,
And, imitating Heav'n, draw good from ill:
Nor let these great researches in my breast
A monument of useless labour rest: 　520
No—let them spread—th' effects let Gotham share,
And reap the harvest of their monarch's care:
Be other times and other countries known,
Only to give fresh blessings to my own.
　Let me, (and may that God to whom I fly, 　525
On whom for needful succour I rely
In this great hour, that glorious God of truth!
Thro' whom I reign, in mercy to my youth

Assist my weakness, and direct me right;
From ev'ry speck which hangs upon the sight   530
Purge my mind's eye, nor let one cloud remain
To spread the shades of error o'er my brain)
Let me, impartial, with unweary'd thought
Try men and things: let me, as monarchs ought,
Examine well on what my pow'r depends;   535
What are the gen'ral principles and ends
Of government; how empire first began:
And wherefore man was rais'd to reign o'er man.

 Let me consider, as from one great source
We see a thousand rivers take their course,   540
Dispers'd, and into diff'rent channels led,
Yet by their parent still supplied and fed,
That government, (tho' branch'd out far and wide,
In various modes to various lands apply'd)
Howe'er it differs in its outward frame,   545
In the main groundwork 's ev'ry where the same;
The same her view, tho' different her plan,
Her grand and gen'ral view the good of man.

 Let me find out, by reason's sacred beams,
What system in itself most perfect seems,   550
Most worthy man, most likely to conduce
To all the purposes of gen'ral use:
Let me find too where, by fair reason try'd,
It fails when to particulars apply'd;
Why in that mode all nations do not join,   555
And chiefly why it cannot suit with mine.

Let me the gradual rise of empires trace,
Till they seem founded on Perfection's base;
Then (for when human things have made their way
To excellence they hasten to decay) 560
Let me, whilst Observation lends her clue,
Step by step to their quick decline pursue,
Enabled by a chain of facts to tell
Not only how they rose but how they fell.

Let me not only the distempers know 565
Which in all states from common causes grow,
But likewise those which, by the will of Fate,
On each peculiar mode of empire wait,
Which in its very constitution lurk,
Too sure at last to do its destin'd work: 570
Let me, forewarn'd, each sign, each system, learn,
That I my people's danger may discern,
Ere 't is too late wish'd health to reassure,
And, if it can be found, find out a cure.

Let me, (tho' great grave brethren of the gown 575
Preach all faith up, and preach all reason down,
Making those jar whom reason meant to join,
And vesting in themselves a right divine)
Let me thro' reason's glass, with searching eye,
Into the depth of that religion pry 580
Which law hath sanction'd: let me find out there
What 's form, what 's essence, what, like vagrant air,
We well may change; and what, without a crime,
Cannot be chang'd to the last hour of time:

Nor let me suffer that outrageous zeal 585
Which without knowledge furious bigots feel,
Fair in pretence, tho' at the heart unsound,
These sep'rate points at random to confound.

 The times have been when priests have dar'd to tread,
Proud and insulting, on their monarch's head;
When, whilst they made religion a pretence, 591
Out of the world they banish'd common sense;
When some soft king, too open to deceit,
Easy and unsuspecting, join'd the cheat,
Dup'd by mock piety, and gave his name 595
To serve the vilest purposes of shame.
Fear not, my People! where no cause of fear
Can justly rise—your king secures you here;
Your king, who scorns the haughty prelate's nod,
Nor deems the voice of priests the voice of God. 600

 Let me, (tho' lawyers may perhaps forbid
Their monarch to behold what they wish hid,
And for the purposes of knavish gain
Would have their trade a mystery remain)
Let me, disdaining all such slavish awe, 605
Dive to the very bottom of the law;
Let me (the weak dead letter left behind)
Search out the principles, the spirit find,
Till from the parts made master of the whole
I see the Constitution's very soul. 610

 Let me, (tho' statesmen will no doubt resist,
And to my eyes present a fearful list

Of men whose wills are opposite to mine,
Of men, great men! determin'd to resign)
Let me (with firmness, which becomes a king, 615
Conscious from what a source my actions spring,
Determin'd not by worlds to be withstood,
When my grand object is my country's good)
Unravel all low ministerial scenes,
Destroy their jobs, lay bare their ways and means,
And trap them step by step; let me well know 621
How places, pensions, and preferments, go;
Why Guilt's provided for when Worth is not,
And why one man of merit is forgot;
Let me in peace, in war, supreme preside, 625
And dare to know my way without a guide.

 Let me, (tho' Dignity, by nature proud,
Retires from view, and swells behind a cloud,
As if the sun shone with less pow'rful ray,
Less grace, less glory, shining ev'ry day, 630
Tho' when she comes forth into public sight,
Unbending as a ghost she stalks upright,
With such an air as we have often seen,
And often laugh'd at in a tragic queen,
Nor at her presence tho' base myriads crook 635
The supple knee, vouchsafes a single look)
Let me (all vain parade, all empty pride,
All terrors of dominion laid aside,
All ornament, and needless helps of art,
All those big looks which speak a little heart) 640

Know (which few kings, alas! have ever known)
How affability becomes a throne,
Destroys all fear, bids love with rev'rence live,
And gives those graces pride can never give.
Let the stern tyrant keep a distant state,　　　645
And hating all men fear return of hate,
Conscious of guilt retreat behind his throne,
Secure from all upbraidings but his own:
Let all my subjects have access to me;
Be my ears open as my heart is free;　　　650
In full fair tide let information flow;
That evil is half cur'd whose cause we know.

And thou, where'er thou art, thou wretched thing!
Who art afraid to look up to a king,
Lay by thy fears—make but thy grievance plain,
And if I not redress thee may my reign　　　655
Close up that very moment—To prevent
The course of Justice from her fair intent
In vain my nearest dearest friend shall plead,
In vain my mother kneel—My soul may bleed, 660
But must not change—When Justice draws the dart,
Tho' it is doom'd to pierce a fav'rite's heart,
'Tis mine to give it force, to give it aim——
I know it duty and I feel it fame.　　　664

THE PROPHECY OF FAMINE.
A SCOTS PASTORAL.
INSCRIBED TO JOHN WILKES, ESQ.

When Cupid first instructs his darts to fly
From the sly corner of some cookmaid's eye,
The stripling raw, just enter'd in his teens,
Receives the wound, and wonders what it means;
His heart, like dripping, melts, and new desire   5
Within him stirs each time she stirs the fire;
Trembling and blushing he the fair one views,
And fain would speak, but cann't:—without a Muse.
  So to the sacred mount he takes his way,
Prunes his young wings and tunes his infant lay,   10
His oaten reed to rural ditties frames,
To flocks and rocks to hills and rills proclaims
In simplest notes and all unpolish'd strains,
The loves of nymphs and eke the loves of swains.
  Clad as your nymphs were always clad of yore,   15
In rustic weeds—a cookmaid now no more—
Beneath an aged oak Lardella lies—
Green moss her couch, her canopy the skies.
From aromatic shrubs the roguish gale   19
Steals young perfumes, and wafts them thro' the vale:
The youth turn'd swain, and skill'd in rustic lays,
Fast by her side his am'rous descant plays.

Herds lowe, flocks bleat, pies chatter, ravens scream,
And the full chorus dies a-down the stream.
The streams, with music freighted, as they pass 25
Present the fair Lardella with a glass,
And Zephyr, to complete the love-sick plan,
Waves his light wings, and serves her for a fan.
    But when maturer Judgment takes the lead
These childish toys on Reason's altar bleed; 30
Form'd after some great man whose name breeds awe,
Whose ev'ry sentence fashion makes a law,
Who on mere credit his vain trophies rears,
And founds his merit on our servile fears;
Then we discard the workings of the heart, 35
And nature's banish'd by mechanic art:
Then, deeply read, our reading must be shown;
Vain is that knowledge which remains unknown;
Then Ostentation marches to our aid,
And letter'd Pride stalks forth in full parade; 40
Beneath their care behold the work refine,
Pointed each sentence, polish'd ev'ry line:
Trifles are dignify'd, and taught to wear
The robes of ancients with a modern air:
Nonsense with classic ornaments is grac'd, 45
And passes current with the stamp of taste.
    Then the rude Theocrite is ransack'd o'er,
And courtly Maro call'd from Mincio's shore;
Sicilian Muses on our mountains roam,
Easy and free, as if they were at home; 50

Nymphs, Naiads, Nereids, Dryads, Satyrs, Fauns,
Sport in our floods and trip it o'er our lawns; [Rome
Flow'rs which once flourish'd fair in Greece and
More fair revive, in England's meads to bloom;
Skies without cloud exotic suns adorn, 55
And roses blush, but blush without a thorn;
Landscapes unknown to dowdy Nature rise,
And new creations strike our wond'ring eyes.

For bards like these, who neither sing nor say,
Grave without thought, and without feeling gay, 60
Whose numbers in one even tenor flow,
Attun'd to pleasure and attun'd to wo,
Who, if plain Commonsense her visit pays,
And mars one couplet in their happy lays,
As at some ghost affrighted, start and stare, 65
And ask the meaning of her coming there.
For bards like these a wreath shall Mason bring,
Lin'd with the softest down of Folly's wing;
In Love's pagoda shall they ever doze,
And Gisbal kindly rock them to repose; 70
My Lord*—to letters as to faith most true—
At once their patron and example too—
Shall quaintly fashion his love-labour'd dreams,
Sigh with sad winds, and weep with weeping streams,
Curious in grief, (for real grief, we know, 75
Is curious to dress up the tale of wo)

* Lyttelton.

From the green umbrage of some Druid's seat
Shall his own works in his own way repeat.
  Me, whom no Muse of heav'nly birth inspires,
No judgment tempers when rash genius fires,   80
Who boast no merit but mere knack of rhyme,
Short gleams of sense, and satire out of time,
Who cannot follow where trim Fancy leads,
By prattling streams o'er flow'r-empurpled meads,
Who often, but without success, have pray'd   85
For apt Alliteration's artful aid,
Who would but cannot, with a master's skill
Coin fine new epithets which mean no ill:
Me, thus uncouth, thus ev'ry way unfit
For pacing poesy and ambling wit,   90
Taste with contempt beholds, nor deigns to place
Amongst the lowest of her favour'd race.
  'Thou, Nature! art my goddess—to thy law
Myself I dedicate—hence, slavish awe,
Which bends to fashion, and obeys the rules   95
Impos'd at first, and since observ'd by fools;
Hence those vile tricks which mar fair Nature's hue,
And bring the sober matron forth to view,
With all that artificial tawdry glare
Which virtue scorns, and none but strumpets wear.
Sick of those pomps, those vanities, that waste   101
Of toil, which critics now mistake for taste,
Of false refinements sick, and labour'd ease,
Which art too thinly veil'd forbids to please,

By Nature's charms (inglorious truth!) subdu'd,
However plain her dress and 'haviour rude,   106
To northern climes my happier course I steer,
Climes where the goddess reigns throughout the year,
Where undisturb'd by Art's rebellious plan
She rules the royal laird and faithful clan.   110

    To that rare soil, where virtues clustering grow,
What mighty blessings doth not England owe!
What waggon-loads of courage, wealth, and sense,
Doth each revolving day import from thence!
To us she gives, disinterested friend!   115
Faith without fraud, and Stewarts without end.
When we prosperity's rich trappings wear,
Come not her gen'rous sons and take a share?
And if, by some disastrous turn of fate,
Change should ensue, and ruin seize the state,   120
Shall we not find, safe in that hallow'd ground,
Such refuge as the holy Martyr found?

    Nor less our debt in science, tho' deny'd
By the weak slaves of prejudice and pride.
Thence came the Ramsays, names of worthy note,
Of whom one paints as well as t' other wrote: 126
Thence Home, disbanded from the sons of pray'r
For loving plays, tho' no dull dean was there;
Thence issu'd forth, at great Macpherson's call,
That old, new, epic pastoral Fingal;   130
Thence Malloch, friend alike of church and state,
Of Christ and Liberty, by grateful Fate

Rais'd to rewards which in a pious reign
All darling infidels should seek in vain;
Thence simple bards, by simple prudence taught,
To this wise Town by simple patrons brought, 136
In simple manner utter simple lays,
And take with simple pensions simple praise.
Waft me, some Muse, to Tweed's inspiring stream,
Where all the little Loves and Graces dream, 140
Where, slowly winding, the dull waters creep,
And seem themselves to own the pow'r of sleep,
Where on the surface lead like feathers swims;
Theee let me bathe my yet unhallow'd limbs,
As once a Syrian bath'd in Jordan's flood, 145
Wash off my native stains, correct that blood
Which mutinies at call of English pride,
And, deaf to prudence, rolls a patriot tide.

From solemn thought, which overhangs the brow
Of patriot Care when things are—God knows how;
From nice trim points, where Honour, slave to rule,
In compliment to Folly plays the fool; 152
From those gay scenes where Mirth exalts his pow'r,
And easy Humour wings the laughing hour;
From those soft better moments when desire 155
Beats high, and all the world of man's on fire;
When mutual ardours of the melting fair
More than repay us for whole years of care,
At Friendship's summons will my Wilkes retreat,
And see, once seen before, that ancient seat, 160

That ancient seat, where Majesty display'd
Her ensigns long before the world was made!
   Mean narrow maxims, which enslave mankind,
Ne'er from its bias warp thy settled mind:
Not dup'd by party, nor Opinion's slave,   165
Those faculties which bounteous Nature gave
Thy honest spirit into practice brings,
Nor courts the smile nor dreads the frown of kings.
Let rude licentious Englishmen comply
With Tumult's voice, and curse they know not why;
Unwilling to condemn, thy soul disdains   171
To wear vile Faction's arbitrary chains,
And strictly weighs, in apprehension clear,
Things as they are, and not as they appear.
With thee good humour tempers lively wit,   175
Enthron'd with Judgment Candour loves to sit,
And Nature gave thee, open to distress,
A heart to pity and a hand to bless.
   Oft' have I heard thee mourn the wretched lot
Of the poor, mean, despis'd, insulted, Scot,   180
Who, might calm reason credit idle tales,
By rancour forg'd where prejudice prevails,
Or starves at home, or practises, thro' fear
Of starving, arts which damn all conscience here.
When scribblers, to the charge by int'rest led,   185
The fierce North-Briton foaming at their head,
Pour forth invectives, deaf to Candour's call,
And injur'd by one alien rail at all;

On northern Pisgah when they take their stand
To mark the weakness of that Holy Land,   190
With needless truths their libels to adorn,
And hang a nation up to public scorn,
Thy gen'rous soul condemns the frantic rage,
And hates the faithful but ill-natur'd page.

    The Scots are poor, cries surly English pride;
True is the charge, nor by themselves deny'd.   196
Are they not then in strictest reason clear
Who wisely come to mend their fortunes here?
If, by low supple arts successful grown,
They sapp'd our vigour to increase their own;   200
If, mean in want, and insolent in pow'r,
They only fawn'd more surely to devour,
Rous'd by such wrongs should Reason take alarm,
And ev'n the Muse for public safety arm?
But if they own ingenuous Virtue's sway,   205
And follow where true Honour points the way;
If they revere the hand by which they 're fed,
And bless the donors for their daily bread,
Or, by vast debts of higher import bound,
Are always humble, always grateful, found;   210
If they, directed by Paul's holy pen,
Become discreetly all things to all men,
That all men may become all things to them,
Envy may hate, but Justice cann't condemn.
" Into our places, states, and beds, they creep;"   215
They 've sense to get what we want sense to keep.

Once, be the hour accurs'd! accurs'd the place!
I ventur'd to blaspheme the chosen race.
Into those traps which men, call'd Patriots, laid,
By specious arts unwarily betray'd,   220
Madly I leagu'd against that sacred earth,
Vile parricide! which gave a parent birth:
But shall I meanly Error's path pursue,
When heav'nly Truth presents her friendly clue?
Once plung'd in ill shall I go farther in?   225
To make the oath was rash, to keep it sin.
Backward I tread the paths I trode before,
And calm Reflection hates what Passion swore.
Converted, (blessed are the souls which know
Those pleasures which from true conversion flow,
Whether to reason, who now rules my breast,   231
Or to pure faith, like Lyttelton and West)
Past crimes to expiate, be my present aim
To raise new trophies to the Scottish name,
To make (what can the proudest Muse do more?)
Ev'n Faction's sons her brighter worth adore; 236
To make her glories, stamp'd with honest rhymes,
In fullest tide roll down to latest times.

    " Presumptuous wretch! and shall a Muse like thine,
" An English Muse! the meanest of the Nine, 240
" Attempt a theme like this? Can her weak strain
" Expect indulgence from the mighty Thane?
" Should he from toils of government retire,
" And for a moment fan the poet's fire;

" Should he, of sciences the moral friend, 245
" Each curious each important search suspend,
" Leave unassisted Hill of herbs to tell,
" And all the wonders of a cockleshell,
" Having the Lord's good grace before his eyes,
" Would not the Home step forth and gain the prize?
" Or if this wreath of honour might adorn 251
" The humble brows of one in England born,
" Presumptuous still thy daring must appear;
" Vain all thy tow'ring hopes whilst I am here."
 Thus spake a form, by silken smile, and tone
Dull and unvary'd, for the Laureate known, 256
Folly's chief friend, Decorum's eldest son,
In ev'ry party found, and yet of none.
This airy substance, this substantial shade,
Abash'd I heard, and with respect obey'd. 260
 From themes too lofty for a bard so mean
Discretion beckons to an humbler scene;
The restless fever of ambition laid,
Calm I retire, and seek the sylvan shade.
Now be the Muse disrob'd of all her pride, 265
Be all the glare of verse by truth supply'd,
And if plain Nature pours a simple strain,
Which Bute may praise and Ossian not disdain,
Ossian! sublimest simplest bard of all,
Whom English infidels Macpherson call, 270
Then round my head shall Honour's ensigns wave,
And pensions mark me for a willing slave.

Two boys, whose birth, beyond all question, springs
From great and glorious tho' forgotten kings,
Shepherds of Scottish lineage, born and bred   275
On the same bleak and barren mountain's head,
By niggard Nature doom'd on the same rocks
To spin out life, and starve themselves and flocks,
Fresh as the morning which, enrob'd in mist,
The mountain's top with usual dulness kiss'd,   280
Jockey and Sawney, to their labours rose;
Soon clad I ween where Nature needs no clothes,
Where, from their youth enur'd to winter-skies,
Dress and her vain refinements they despise.

  Jockey, whose manly high-bon'd cheeks to crown,
With freckles spotted flam'd the golden down,   286
With meikle art could on the bagpipes play,
Ev'n from the rising to the setting day:
Sawney as long without remorse could bawl
Home's madrigals, and ditties from Fingal: 290
Oft' at his strains, all natural tho' rude,
The Highland lass forgot her want of food,
And, whilst she scratch'd her lover into rest,
Sunk pleas'd tho' hungry on her Sawney's breast.

  Far as the eye could reach no tree was seen,   295
Earth clad in russet scorn'd the lively green:
The plague of locusts they secure defy,
For in three hours a grashopper must die:
No living thing, whate'er its food, feasts there
But the chameleon, who can feast on air.   300

No birds except as birds of passage flew;
No bee was known to hum, no dove to coo:
No streams, as amber smooth, as amber clear,
Were seen to glide, or heard to warble here:
Rebellion's spring, which thro' the country ran, 305
Furnish'd with bitter draughts the steady clan:
No flow'rs embalm'd the air but one White Rose,
Which on the tenth of June by instinct blows,
By instinct blows at morn, and when the shades
Of drizzly eve prevail by instinct fades. 310

 One, and but one, poor solitary cave,
Too sparing of her favours, Nature gave;
That one alone (hard tax on Scottish pride!)
Shelter at once for man and beast supply'd.
Their snares without entangling briers spread, 315
And thistles, arm'd against the invader's head,
Stood in close ranks, all entrance to oppose,
Thistles! now held more precious than the Rose.
All creatures which, on Nature's earliest plan,
Were form'd to loathe and to be loath'd by man, 320
Which ow'd their birth to nastiness and spite,
Deadly to touch, and hateful to the sight;
Creatures, which when admitted in the ark
Their saviour shunn'd, and rankled in the dark,
Found place within. Marking her noisome road 325
With poison's trail, here crawl'd the bloated toad;
There webs were spread of more than common size,
And half-starv'd spiders prey'd on half-starv'd flies:

In quest of food efts strove in vain to crawl;
Slugs pinch'd with hunger smear'd the slimy wall:
The cave around with hissing serpents rung; 331
On the damp roof unhealthy vapour hung;
And Famine, by her children always known,
As proud as poor, here fix'd her native throne.

   Here, for the sullen sky was overcast, 335
And summer shrunk beneath a wintry blast,
A native blast, which, arm'd with hail and rain,
Beat unrelenting on the naked swain,
The boys for shelter made: behind the sheep,
Of which those shepherds ev'ry day take keep, 340
Sickly crept on, and, with complainings rude,
On Nature seem'd to call and bleat for food.

   JOCKEY. Sith to this cave by tempest we're con-
And within ken our flocks, under the wind, [fin'd,
Safe from the pelting of this per'lous storm, 345
Are laid emong yon' thistles, dry and warm,
What, Sawney, if by shepherd's art we try
To mock the rigour of this cruel sky?
What if we tune some merry roundelay?
Well dost thou sing, nor ill doth Jockey play. 350

   SAWNEY. Ah! Jockey, ill advisest thou, I wis,
To think of songs at such a time as this:
Sooner shall herbage crown these barren rocks,
Sooner shall fleeces clothe these ragged flocks,
Sooner shall want seize shepherds of the south, 355
And we forget to live from hand to mouth,

Than Sawney, out of season, shall impart
The songs of gladness with an aching heart.

 JOCKEY. Still have I known thee for a silly swain;
Of things past help what boots it to complain? 360
Nothing but mirth can conquer Fortune's spite;
No sky is heavy if the heart be light:
Patience is sorrow's salve: what cann't be cur'd,
So Donald right areeds, must be endur'd.

 SAWNEY. Full silly swain, I wot, is Jockey now; 365
How didst thou bear thy Maggy's falsehood? how,
When with a foreign loon she stole away,
Didst thou forswear thy pipe and shepherd's lay?
Where was thy boasted wisdom then, when I
Apply'd those proverbs which you now apply? 370

 JOCKEY. O she was bonny! all the Highlands round
Was there a rival to my Maggy found?
More precious (tho' that precious is to all)
Than the rare med'cine which we Brimstone call,
Or that choice plant, so grateful to the nose, 375
Which in I know not what far country grows,
Was Maggy unto me: dear do I rue
A lass so fair should ever prove untrue.

 SAWNEY. Whether with pipe or song to charm the ear,
Thro' all the land did Jamie find a peer?
Curs'd be that year by ev'ry honest Scot, 381
And in the shepherds kalendar forgot,
That fatal year, when Jamie, hapless swain!
In evil hour forsook the peaceful plain:

       L ij

Jamie, when our young laird discreetly fled, 385
Was seiz'd, and hang'd till he was dead, dead, dead.

JOCKEY. Full sorely may we all lament that day,
For all were losers in the deadly fray;
Five brothers had I on the Scottish plains, 389
Well dost thou know were none more hopeful swains;
Five brothers there I lost, in manhood's pride,
Two in the field, and three on gibbets dy'd:
Ah! silly swains! to follow war's alarms;
Ah! what hath shepherd's life to do with arms? 394

SAWNEY. Mention it not—There saw I strangers
In all the honours of our ravish'd Plaid; [clad
Saw the Ferrara, too, our nation's pride,
Unwilling grace the awkward victor's side.
There fell our choicest youth, and from that day
Mote never Sawney tune the merry lay; 400
Bless'd those which fell! curs'd those which still sur-
To mourn Fifteen renew'd in Forty-five. [vive!

Thus plain'd the boys, when from her throne of
With boils emboss'd, and overgrown with scurf, [turf
Vile humours, which in life's corrupted well 405
Mix'd at the birth not abstinence could quell,
Pale Famine rear'd the head; her eager eyes,
Where hunger ev'n to madness seem'd to rise,
Speaking aloud her throes and pangs of heart,
Strain'd to get loose, and from their orbs to start: 410
Her hollow cheeks were each a deep sunk cell,
Where wretchedness and horror lov'd to dwell:

With double rows of useless teeth supply'd,
Her mouth from ear to ear extended wide,
Which when for want of food her entrails pin'd 415
She op'd, and, cursing, swallow'd nought but wind:
All shrivell'd was her skin; and here and there,
Making their way by force, her bones lay bare:
Such filthy sight to hide from human view
O'er her foul limbs a tatter'd Plaid she threw. 420
    " Cease," cry'd the goddess, " cease, despairing
And from a parent hear what Jove ordains. [swains!
    Pent in this barren corner of the isle,
Where partial Fortune never deign'd to smile,
Like Nature's bastards, reaping for our share 425
What was rejected by the lawful heir;
Unknown amongst the nations of the earth,
Or only known to raise contempt and mirth;
Long free, because the race of Roman braves
Thought it not worth their while to make us slaves,
Then into bondage by that nation brought 431
Whose ruin we for ages vainly sought,
Whom still with unslak'd hate we view, and still,
The pow'r of mischief lost, retain the will;
Consider'd as the refuse of mankind, 435
A mass till the last moment left behind,
Which frugal Nature doubted, as it lay,
Whether to stamp with life or throw away;
Which, form'd in haste, was planted in this nook,
But never enter'd in Creation's book, 440

Branded as traitors, who for love of gold,
Would sell their god, as once their king they sold;
Long have we borne this mighty weight of ill,
These vile injurious taunts, and bear them still;
But times of happier note are now at hand,　445
And the full promise of a better land:
There, like the sons of Isr'el, having trode
For the fix'd term of years ordain'd by God,
A barren desert, we shall seize rich plains,
Where milk with honey flows, and plenty reigns: 450
With some few natives join'd, some pliant few,
Who worship int'rest, and our track pursue;
There shall we, tho' the wretched people grieve,
Ravage at large, nor ask the owners leave.

 For us the earth shall bring forth her increase; 455
For us the flocks shall wear a golden fleece;
Fat beeves shall yield us dainties not our own,
And the grape bleed a nectar yet unknown:
For our advantage shall their harvests grow,
And Scotsmen reap what they disdain'd to sow: 460
For us the sun shall climb the eastern hill;
For us the rain shall fall, the dew distil:
When to our wishes Nature cannot rise,
Art shall be tax'd to grant us fresh supplies;
His brawny arm shall drudging Labour strain, 465
And for our pleasure suffer daily pain:
Trade shall for us exert her utmost pow'rs,
Hers all the toil, and all the profit ours:

For us the oak shall from his native steep
Descend, and fearless travel thro' the deep; 470
The sail of commerce, for our use unfurl'd,
Shall waft the treasures of each distant world:
For us sublimer heights shall science reach;
For us their statesmen plot, their churchmen preach:
Their noblest limbs of counsel we'll disjoint, 475
And, mocking, new ones of our own appoint:
Devouring War, imprison'd in the north,
Shall at our call in horrid pomp break forth,
And when, his chariot wheels with thunder hung,
Fell Discord braying with her brazen tongue, 480
Death in the van, with Anger, Hate, and Fear,
And Desolation stalking in the rear,
Revenge, by Justice guided, in his train,
He drives impet'ous o'er the trembling plain,
Shall at our bidding quit his lawful prey, 485
And to meek, gentle, gen'rous Peace give way.

 Think not, my sons! that this so bless'd estate
Stands at a distance on the roll of Fate;
Already big with hopes of future sway,
Ev'n from this cave I scent my destin'd prey. 490
Think not that this dominion o'er a race,
Whose former deeds shall time's last annals grace,
In the rough face of peril must be sought,
And with the lives of thousands dearly bought:
No—fool'd by cunning, by that happy art 495
Which laughs to scorn the blund'ring hero's heart,

Into the snare shall our kind neighbours fall,
With open eyes, and fondly give us all.
   When Rome, to prop her sinking empire, bore
Their choicest levies to a foreign shore,   500
What if we seiz'd, like a destroying flood,
Their widow'd plains, and fill'd the realm with blood,
Gave an unbounded loose to manly rage,
And, scorning mercy, spar'd nor sex nor age?
When, for our interest too mighty grown,   505
Monarchs of warlike bent possess'd the throne,
What if we strove divisions to foment,
And spread the flames of civil discontent,
Assisted those who 'gainst their king made head,
And gave the traitors refuge when they fled?   510
When restless Glory bade her sons advance,
And pitch'd her standard in the fields of France,
What if, disdaining oaths, an empty sound,
By which our nation never shall be bound,
Bravely we taught unmuzzled War to roam   515
Thro' the weak land, and brought cheap laurels home?
When the bold traitors leagu'd for the defence
Of law, religion, liberty, and sense,
When they against their lawful monarch rose,
And dar'd the Lord's anointed to oppose,   520
What if we still rever'd the banish'd race,
And strove the royal vagrants to replace,
With fierce rebellions shook th' unsettled state,
And greatly dar'd, tho' cross'd by partial Fate?   524

These facts, which might, where wisdom held the sway,
Awake the very stones to bar our way,
There shall be nothing, nor one trace remain
In the dull region of an English brain:
Bless'd with that faith which mountains can remove,
First they shall dupes, next saints, last martyrs, prove.

 Already is this game of Fate begun   531
Under the sanction of my darling son;
That son, of nature royal as his name,
Is destin'd to redeem our race from shame:
His boundless pow'r, beyond example great,   535
Shall make the rough way smooth, the crooked straight;
Shall for our ease the raging floods restrain,
And sink the mountain level to the plain.
Discord, whom in a cavern under ground
With massy fetters their late patriot bound,   540
Where her own flesh the furious hag might tear,
And vent her curses to the vacant air,
Where, that she never might be heard of more,
He planted Loyalty to guard the door,
For better purpose shall our chief release,   545
Disguise her for a time, and call her Peace.

 Lur'd by that name, fine engine of deceit!
Shall the weak English help themselves to cheat;
To gain our love, with honours shall they grace
The old adherents of the Stewart race,   550
Who pointed out, no matter by what name,
Tories or Jacobites, are still the same:

To sooth our rage, the temporising brood
Shall break the ties of truth and gratitude;
Against their saviour venom'd falsehoods frame, 555
And brand with calumny their William's name:
To win our grace (rare argument of wit!)
To our untainted faith shall they commit
(Our faith which, in extremest perils try'd,
Disdain'd and still disdains to change her side) 560
That sacred Majesty they all approve,
Who most enjoys and best deserves their love." 562

THE TIMES.

The time hath been, a boyish blushing time,
When modesty was scarcely held a crime,
When the most wicked had some touch of grace,
And trembled to meet Virtue face to face;
When those who, in the cause of sin grown gray, 5
Had serv'd her without grudging day by day,
Were yet so weak an awkward shame to feel,
And strove that glorious service to conceal:
We, better bred, and than our sires more wise,
Such paltry narrowness of soul despise, 10
To virtue ev'ry mean pretence disclaim,
Lay bare our crimes, and glory in our shame.

    Time was, ere Temperance had fled the realm,
Ere Luxury sat guttling at the helm
From meal to meal, without one moment's space 15
Reserv'd for bus'ness, or allow'd for grace;
Ere vanity had so far conquer'd sense
To make us all wild rivals in expence,
To make one fool strive to outvie another,
And ev'ry coxcomb dress against his brother; 20
Ere banish'd Industry had left our shores,
And Labour was by Pride kick'd out of doors;
Ere Idleness prevail'd sole queen in courts,
Or only yielded to a rage for sports;

Ere each weak mind was with externals caught, 25
And dissipation held the place of thought;
Ere gambling lords in vice so far were gone
To cog the die, and bid the sun look on;
Ere a great nation, not less just than free,
Was made a beggar by Economy; 30
Ere rugged Honesty was out of vogue;
Ere Fashion stamp'd her sanction on the rogue;
Time was that men had conscience, that they made
Scruples to owe what never could be paid.
Was one then found, however high his name, 35
So far above his fellows damn'd to shame,
Who dar'd abuse and falsify his trust,
Who being great yet dar'd to be unjust?
Shunn'd like a plague, or but at distance view'd,
He walk'd the crowded streets in solitude; 40
Nor could his rank or station in the land
Bribe one mean knave to take him by the hand.
Such rigid maxims (O might such revive
To keep expiring Honesty alive!)
Made rogues, all other hopes of fame deny'd, 45
Not just thro' principle but just thro' pride.

   Our times more polish'd wear a diff'rent face;
Debts are an honour, payment a disgrace.
Men of weak minds, high plac'd on folly's list,
May gravely tell us trade cannot subsist, 50
Nor all those thousands who 're in trade employ'd,
If faith 'twixt man and man is once destroy'd.

Why—be it so—we in that point accord,
But what is trade and tradesmen to a lord?
  Faber from day to day, from year to year, 55
Hath had the cries of tradesmen in his ear,
Of tradesmen by his villany betray'd,
And, vainly seeking justice, bankrupts made.
What is 't to Faber? lordly as before
He sits at ease, and lives to ruin more: 60
Fix'd at his door, as motionless as stone,
Begging, but only begging for their own,
Unheard they stand, or only heard by those,
Those slaves in livery, who mock their woes.
What is 't to Faber? he continues great, 65
Lives on in grandeur, and runs out in state.
The helpless widow, wrung with deep despair,
In bitterness of soul pours forth her pray'r,
Hugging her starving babes with streaming eyes,
And calls down vengeance, vengeance from the skies.
What is 't to Faber? he stands safe and clear, 71
Heav'n can commence no legal action here;
And on his breast a mighty plate he wears,
A plate more firm than triple brass, which bears
The name of Privilege, 'gainst vulgar awe; 75
He feels no conscience, and he fears no law.
  Nor think, acquainted with small knaves alone,
Who have not shame outliv'd and grace outgrown,
The great world hidden from thy reptile view,
That on such men, to whom contempt is due, 80

Volume III. M

Contempt shall fall, and their vile author's name
Recorded stand thro' all the land of shame.
No—to his porch, like Persians to the sun,
Behold contending crowds of courtiers run;
See, to his aid what noble troops advance,   85
All sworn to keep his crimes in countenance:
Nor wonder at it—they partake the charge,
As small their conscience and their debts as large.

Propp'd by such clients, and without control
From all that 's honest in the human soul;   90
In grandeur mean, with insolence unjust,
Whilst none but knaves can praise and fools will
Caress'd and courted, Faber seems to stand [trust,
A mighty pillar in a guilty land.
And (a sad truth, to which succeeding times   95
Will scarce give credit when 't is told in rhymes)
Did not strict Honour with a jealous eye
Watch round the throne, did not true Piety
(Who, link'd with Honour for the noblest ends,
Ranks none but honest men amongst her friends)
Forbid us to be crush'd with such a weight,   101
He might in time be minister of state.

But why enlarge I on such petty crimes?
They might have shock'd the faith of former times,
But now are held as nothing—We begin   105
Where our sires ended, and improve in sin;
Rack our invention, and leave nothing new
In vice and folly for our sons to do.

Nor deem this censure hard; there 's not a place
Most consecrate to purposes of grace
Which Vice hath not polluted; none so high,
But with bold pinion she hath dar'd to fly,
And build there for her pleasure; none so low,
But she hath crept into it, made it know
And feel her pow'r: in courts, in camps, she reigns,
O'er sober citizens and simple swains;
Ev'n in our temples she hath fix'd her throne,
And 'bove God's holy altars plac'd her own.
  More to increase the horror of our state,
To make her empire lasting as 'tis great,
To make us, in full-grown perfection, feel
Curses which neither art nor time can heal,
All shame discarded, all remains of pride,
Meanness sits crown'd, and triumphs by her side;
Meanness, who gleans out of the human mind
Those few good seeds which Vice had left behind,
Those seeds which might in time to virtue tend,
And leaves the soul without a pow'r to mend;
Meanness, at sight of whom, with brave disdain,
The breast of Manhood swells, but swells in vain,
Before whom Honour makes a forc'd retreat,
And Freedom is compell'd to quit her seat;
Meanness, which like that mark by bloody Cain
Borne in his forehead for a brother slain,
God in his great and all-subduing rage
Ordains the standing mark of this vile age.

The venal hero trucks his fame for gold,
The patriot's virtue for a place is sold;
The statesman bargains for his country's shame,
And for preferment priests their God disclaim.   140
Worn out with lust, her day of lech'ry o'er,
The mother trains the daughter which she bore
In her own paths; the father aids the plan,
And, when the innocent is ripe for man,
Sells her to some old lecher for a wife,   145
And makes her an adulteress for life;
Or in the Papers bids his name appear,
And advertises for a L——:
Husband and wife (whom Av'rice must applaud)
Agree to save the charge of pimp and bawd: 150
These parts they play themselves, a frugal pair,
And share the infamy the gain to share,
Well pleas'd to find, when they the profits tell,
That they have play'd the whore and rogue so well.
 Nor are these things (which might imply a spark
Of shame still left) transacted in the dark: 156
No—to the public they are open laid,
And carry'd on like any other trade,
Scorning to mince damnation, and too proud
To work the works of darkness in a cloud.   160
In fullest vigour Vice maintains her sway;
Free are her marts, and open at noon-day.
Meanness, now wed to Impudence, no more
In darkness skulks, and trembles, as of yore,

When the light breaks upon her coward eye, 165
Boldly she stalks on earth, and to the sky
Lifts her proud head, nor fears lest time abate,
And turn her husband's love to canker'd hate,
Since Fate, to make them more sincerely one,
Hath crown'd their loves with Montague their son;
A son so like his dam, so like his sire, 171
With all the mother's craft, the father's fire,
An image so express in ev'ry part,
So like in all bad qualities of heart,
That, had they fifty children, he alone 175
Would stand as heir-apparent to the throne.

 With our own island-vices not content,
We rob our neighbours on the continent,
Dance Europe round, and visit ev'ry court,
To ape their follies and their crimes import; 180
To diff'rent lands for diff'rent sins we roam,
And, richly freighted, bring our cargo home,
Nobly industrious to make Vice appear
In her full state, and perfect only here.

 To Holland, where politeness ever reigns, 185
Where primitive sincerity remains,
And makes a stand; where Freedom in her course
Hath left her name, tho' she hath lost her force
In that as other lands; where simple Trade
Was never in the garb of Fraud array'd; 190
Where Av'rice never dar'd to shew his head;
Where, like a smiling cherub, Mercy led

By Reason blesses the sweet-blooded race,
And Cruelty could never find a place;
To Holland for that Charity we roam   195
Which happily begins and ends at home.

 France, in return for peace and pow'r restor'd,
For all those countries which the hero's sword
Unprofitably purchas'd, idly thrown
Into her lap, and made once more her own;   200
France hath afforded large and rich supplies
Of vanities full trimm'd, of polish'd lies,
Of soothing flatteries, which thro' the ears
Steal to and melt the heart, of slavish fears
Which break the spirit, and of abject fraud— 205
For which, alas! we need not send abroad.

 Spain gives us pride—which Spain to all the earth
May largely give, nor fear herself a dearth—
Gives us that jealousy which, born of Fear
And mean Distrust, grows not by Nature here—
Gives us that superstition which pretends   211
By the worst means to serve the best of ends—
That cruelty which, stranger to the brave,
Dwells only with the coward and the slave,
That cruelty which led her Christian bands   215
With more than savage rage o'er savage lands
Bade her, without remorse, whole countries thin,
And hold of nought but mercy as a sin.

 Italia, nurse of ev'ry softer art,
Who feigning to refine unmans the heart;   220

Who lays the realms of Sense and Virtue waste;
Who mars whilst she pretends to mend our taste;
Italia, to complete and crown our shame,
Sends us a fiend, and Legion is his name.
The farce of greatness without being great, 225
Pride without pow'r, titles without estate,
Souls without vigour, bodies without force,
Hate without cause, revenge without remorse,
Dark mean revenge, murder without defence,
Jealousy without love, sound without sense, 230
Mirth without humour, without wit grimace,
Faith without reason, Gospel without grace,
Zeal without knowledge, without nature art,
Men without manhood, women without heart;
Half-men, who, dry and pithless, are debarr'd 235
From man's best joys--no sooner made than marr'd--
Half-men, whom many a rich and noble dame,
To serve her lust and yet secure her fame,
Keeps on high diet, as we capons feed,
To glut our appetites at last decreed; 240
Women who dance in postures so obscene,
They might awaken shame in Aretine;
Who, when retir'd from the day's piercing light,
They celebrate the mysteries of Night,
Might make the Muses, in a corner plac'd 245
To view their monstrous lusts, deem Sappho chaste:
These, and a thousand follies rank as these,
A thousand faults, ten thousand fools, who please

Our pall'd and sickly taste, ten thousand knaves,
Who serve our foes as spies and us as slaves, 250
Why by degrees, and unperceiv'd, prepare
Our necks for chains which they already wear,
Madly we entertain, at the expense
Of fame, of virtue, taste, and common sense.

 Nor stop we here—the soft luxurious east, 255
Where man, his soul degraded, from the beast
In nothing diff'rent but in shape we view,
They walk on four legs, and he walks on two,
Attracts our eye, and flowing from that source
Sins of the blackest character, sins worse 260
Than all her plagues, which truly to unfold
Would make the best blood in my veins run cold,
And strike all manhood dead, which but to name
Would call up in my cheeks the marks of shame;
Sins, if such sins can be, which shut out grace, 265
Which for the guilty leave no hope, no place,
Ev'n in God's mercy; sins 'gainst Nature's plan
Possess the land at large, and man for man
Burn in those fires which hell alone could raise
To make him more than damn'd; which in the days
Of punishment, when guilt becomes her prey, 271
With all her tortures she can scarce repay.

 Be grace shut out, be mercy deaf, let God
With tenfold terrors arm that dreadful nod
Which speaks them lost, and sentenc'd to despair;
Distending wide her jaws, let Hell prepare, 276

For those who thus offend amongst mankind,
A fire more fierce, and tortures more refin'd : 278
On earth, which groans beneath their monstrous
On earth, alas ! they meet a different fate; [weight,
And whilst the laws, false grace, false mercy, shown,
Are taught to wear a softness not their own,
Men whom the beasts would spurn, should they appear
Amongst the honest herd, find refuge here.

  No longer by vain fear or shame controll'd, 285
From long, too long, security grown bold,
Mocking rebuke, they brave it in our streets,
And Lumley ev'n at noon his mistress meets :
So public in their crimes, so daring grown,
They almost take a pride to have them known, 290
And each unnat'ral villain scarce endures
To make a secret of his vile amours.
Go where we will, at ev'ry time and place,
Sodom confronts and stares us in the face;
They ply in public at our very doors, 295
And take the bread from much more honest whores;
Those who are mean high paramours secure,
And the rich guilty screen the guilty poor;
The sin too proud to feel from reason awe,
And those who practise it too great for law. 300

  Woman ! the pride and happiness of man,
Without whose soft endearments Nature's plan
Had been a blank, and life not worth a thought;
Woman ! by all the Loves and Graces taught,

With softest arts, and sure tho' hidden skill, 305
To humanize and mould us to her will;
Woman! with more than common grace form'd here,
With the persuasive language of a tear
To melt the rugged temper of our isle,
Or win us to her purpose with a smile; 310
Woman! by Fate the quickest spur decreed,
The fairest, best, reward of ev'ry deed
Which bears the stamp of honour, at whose name
Our ancient heroes caught a quicker flame,
And dar'd beyond belief, whilst o'er the plain, 315
Spurning the carcasses of princes slain,
Confusion proudly strode, whilst Horror blew
The fatal trump, and Death stalk'd full in view;
Woman is out of date, a thing thrown by,
As having lost its use: no more the eye, 320
With female beauty caught, in wild amaze
Gazes entranc'd, and could for ever gaze;
No more the heart, that seat where Love resides,
Each breath drawn quick and short, in fuller tides
Life posting thro' the veins, each pulse on fire, 325
And the whole body tingling with desire,
Pants for those charms which Virtue might engage
To break his vow and thaw the frost of Age,
Bidding each trembling nerve, each muscle, strain,
And giving pleasure which is almost pain. 330
Women are kept for nothing but the breed;
For pleasure we must have a Ganymede,

A fine fresh Hylas, a delicious boy,
To serve our purposes of beastly joy !
   Fairest of nymphs where ev'ry nymph is fair, 335
Whom Nature form'd with more than common care,
With more than common care whom Art improv'd,
And both declar'd most worthy to be lov'd,
——— neglected wanders, whilst a crowd
Pursue and consecrate the steps ——— 340
She, hapless maid ! born in a wretched hour,
Wastes life's gay prime in vain, like some fair flow'r
Sweet in its scent, and lively in its hue,
Which withers on the stalk from whence it grew,
And dies uncropp'd; whilst he, admir'd, caress'd,
Belov'd, and ev'ry where a welcome guest, 346
With brutes of rank and fortune plays the whore,
For this unnat'ral lost a common sew'r.
   Dine with Apicius—at his sumpt'ous board
Find all the world of dainties can afford— 350
And yet (so much distemper'd spirits pall
The sickly appetite) amidst them all
Apicius finds no joy, but whilst he carves
For ev'ry guest the landlord sits and starves.
   The forest haunch, fine, fat, in flavour high, 355
Kept to a moment, smokes before his eye,
But smokes in vain ; his heedless eye runs o'er,
And loathes what he had deify'd before :
The turtle, of a great and glorious size,
  Worth its own weight in gold, a mighty prize, 360

For which a man of taste all risks would run,
Itself a feast, and ev'ry dish in one;
The turtle in luxurious pomp comes in,
Kept, kill'd, cut up, prepar'd, and dress'd, by Quin;
In vain it comes, in vain lies full in view; 365
As Quin hath dress'd it he may eat it too;
Apicius cannot— When the glass goes round,
Quick-circling, and the roofs with mirth resound,
Sober he sits, and silent—all alone
Tho' in a crowd; and to himself scarce known, 370
On grief he feeds; nor friends can cure nor wine
Suspend his cares, and make him cease to pine.

 Why mourns Apicius thus? why runs his eye
Heedless o'er delicates which from the sky   [wish
Might call down Jove? Where now his gen'rous
That, to invent a new and better dish, 376
The world might burn and all mankind expire,
So he might roast a phœnix at the fire?
Why swims that eye in tears which thro' a race
Of sixty years ne'er show'd one sign of grace? 380
Why feels that heart which never felt before?
Why doth that pamper'd glutton eat no more,
Who only liv'd to eat, his stomach pall'd,
And drown'd in floods of sorrow? Hath Fate call'd
His father from the grave to second life? 385
Hath Clodius on his hands return'd his wife?
Or hath the law, by strictest justice taught,
Compell'd him to restore the dow'r she brought?

Hath some bold creditor, against his will,
Brought in and forc'd him to discharge a bill 390
Where eating had no share? hath some vain wench
Run out his wealth and forc'd him to retrench?
Hath any rival glutton got the start,
And beat him in his own luxurious art?
Bought cates for which Apicius could not pay, 395
Or dress'd old dainties in a newer way?
Hath his cook, worthy to be flain with rods,
Spoil'd a dish fit to entertain the gods?
Or hath some varlet, cross'd by cruel Fate,
Thrown down the price of empires in a plate? 400

 None, none of these—his servants all are try'd,
So sure, they walk on ice and never slide;
His cook, an acquisition made in France,
Might put a Cloe out of countenance;
Nor, tho' old Holles still maintains his stand, 405
Hath he one rival glutton in the land.
Women are all the objects of his hate;
His debts are all unpaid, and yet his state
In full security and triumph held,
Unless for once a knave should be expell'd: 410
His wife is still a whore, and in his pow'r,
The woman gone, he still retains the dow'r:
Sound in the grave (thanks to his filial care
Which mix'd the draught and kindly sent him there)
His father sleeps, and till the last trump shake 415
The corners of the earth, shall not awake.

Volume III.

Whence flows this sorrow then? Behind his chair
Didst thou not see, deck'd with a solitaire,
Which on his bare breast glitt'ring play'd, and grac'd
With nicest ornaments, a stripling plac'd,   420
A smooth smug stripling, in life's fairest prime?
Didst thou not mind, too, how from time to time
The monstrous lecher, tempted to despise
All other dainties, thither turn'd his eyes?
How he seem'd inly to reproach us all,   425
Who strove his fix'd attention to recall,
And how he wish'd, ev'n at the time of grace,
Like Janus, to have had a double face?
His cause of grief behold in that fair boy;
Apicius dotes, and Corydon is coy.   430

Vain and unthinking stripling! when the glass
Meets thy too curious eye, and, as you pass
Flatt'ring, presents in smiles thy image there,
Why dost thou bless the gods who made thee fair?
Blame their large bounties, and with reason blame;
Curse, curse thy beauty, for it leads to shame: 436
When thy hot lord, to work thee to his end,
Bids show'rs of gold into thy breast descend,
Suspect his gifts, nor the vile giver trust;
They 're baits for virtue, and smell strong of lust.
On those gay gaudy trappings which adorn   441
The temple of thy body look with scorn;
View them with horror; they pollution mean
And deepest ruin. Thou hast often seen

From 'mongst the herd the fairest and the best 445
Carefully singled out, and richly drest,
With grandeur mock'd, for sacrifice decreed,
Only in greater pomp at last to bleed.
Be warn'd in time, the threaten'd danger shun,
To stay a moment is to be undone. 450
What tho', temptation proof, thy virtue shine,
Nor bribes can move nor arts can undermine?
All other methods failing, one resource
Is still behind, and thou must yield to force.
Paint to thyself the horrors of a rape, 455
Most strongly paint, and whilst thou canst escape:
Mind not his promises—they 're made in sport—
Made to be broke—was he not bred at court?
Trust not his honour, he 's a man of birth;
Attend not to his oaths—they 're made on earth, 460
Not register'd in heav'n—he mocks at grace,
And in his creed God never found a place—
Look not for Conscience—for he knows her not,
So long a stranger she is quite forgot—
Nor think thyself in law secure and firm— 465
Thy master is a lord and thou a worm,
A poor mean reptile never meant to think,
Who being well supply'd with meat and drink,
And suffer'd just to crawl from place to place,
Must serve his lusts, and think he does thee grace.

   Fly then whilst yet 't is in thy pow'r to fly. 471
But whither canst thou go? on whom rely

For wish'd protection? Virtue 's sure to meet
An armed host of foes in ev'ry street.
What boots it of Apicius fearful grown   475
Headlong to fly into the arms of Stone?
Or why take refuge in the house of pray'r,
If sure to meet with an Apicius there?
Trust not old age, which will thy faith betray;
Saint Socrates is still a goat tho' gray: 480
Trust not green youth; Florio will scarce go down,
And at eighteen hath surfeited the Town:
Trust not to rakes—alas! 't is all pretence—
They take up raking only as a fence
'Gainst common fame—place H—— in thy view,
He keeps one whore as Barrowby kept two: 486
Trust not to marriage— T—— took a wife,
Who chaste as Dian might have pass'd her life,
Had she not, far more prudent in her aim,
(To propagate the honours of his name,   490
And save expiring titles) taken care,
Without his knowledge, to provide an heir:
Trust not to marriage, in mankind unread;
S——'s a marry'd man, and S—— new wed.

 Wouldst thou be safe? society forswear,   495
Fly to the desert, and seek shelter there;
Herd with the brutes—they follow Nature's plan—
There 's not one brute so dangerous as man
In Afric's wilds—'mongst them that refuge find
Which lust denies thee here among mankind: 500

Renounce thy name, thy nature, and no more
Pique thy vain pride on manhood: on all four
Walk, as you see those honest creatures do,
And quite forget that once you walk'd on two.
 But if the thoughts of solitude alarm,   505
And social life hath one remaining charm;
If still thou art to jeopardy decreed
Amongst the monsters of Augusta's breed,
Lay by thy sex thy safety to procure,
Put off the man, from men to live secure;   510
Go forth a woman to the public view,
And with their garb assume their manners too.
Had the light-footed Greek of Chiron's school
Been wise enough to keep this single rule,
The maudlin hero, like a puling boy   515
Robb'd of his plaything, on the plains of Troy
Had never blubber'd at Patroclus' tomb,
And plac'd his minion in his mistress' room.
Be not in this than catamites more nice,
Do that for virtue which they do for vice—   520
Thus shalt thou pass untainted life's gay bloom,
Thus stand uncourted in the drawing-room;
At midnight thus untempted walk the street,
And run no danger but of being beat.
 Where is the mother whose officious zeal,   525
Discreetly judging what her daughters feel
By what she felt herself in days of yore,
Against that lecher man makes fast the door?

Who not permits, ev'n for the sake of pray'r,
A priest uncastrated to enter there, 530
Nor (could her wishes and her care prevail)
Would suffer in the house a fly that 's male?
Let her discharge her cares, throw wide her doors,
Her daughters cannot if they would be whores;
Nor can a man be found, as Times now go, 535
Who thinks it worth his while to make them so.

 Tho' they more fresh more lively than the morn,
And brighter than the noonday sun, adorn
The works of Nature; tho' the mother's grace
Revives improv'd in ev'ry daughter's face, 540
Undisciplin'd in dull Discretion's rules,
Untaught and undebauch'd by boarding-schools,
Free and unguarded let them range the Town,
Go forth at random, and run pleasure down,
Start where she will; discard all taint of fear, 545
Nor think of danger when no danger 's near,
Watch not their steps—they're safe without thy care,
Unless, like Jennets, they conceive by air,
And ev'ry one of them may die a nun,
Unless they breed like carrion in the sun. 550
Men, dead to pleasure as they 're dead to grace,
Against the law of Nature set their face,
The grand primeval law, and seem combin'd
To stop the propagation of mankind.
Vile pathics read the Marriage Act with pride, 555
And fancy that the law is on their side.

Broke down, and strength a stranger to his bed,
Old L——, tho' yet alive, is dead;
T—— lives no more, or lives not to our isle;
No longer bless'd with a Cz———'s smile;   560
'T—— is at P——— disgrac'd,
And M—— grown gray perforce grows chaste;
Not to the credit of our modest race
Rises one stallion to supply their place.
A maidenhead, which twenty years ago   565
In mid December the rank fly would blow
Tho' closely kept, now when the Dogstar's heat
Inflames the marrow, in the very street
May lie untouch'd, left for the worms by those
Who daintily pass by and hold their nose.   570
Poor plain Concupiscence is in disgrace,
And simple Lech'ry dares not show her face,
Lest she be sent to Bridewell: bankrupts made,
To save their fortunes bawds leave off that trade 574
Which first had left off them; to Well-close Square
Fine fresh young strumpets (for Dodd preaches there)
Throng for subsistence: pimps no longer thrive,
And pensions only keep L—— alive.
 Where is the mother who thinks all her pain
And all her jeopardy of travail gain   580
When a manchild is born, thinks ev'ry pray'r
Paid to the full, and answer'd in an heir?
Shortsighted Woman! little doth she know
 What streams of sorrow from that source may flow;

Little suspect, while she surveys her boy, 585
Her young Narcissus, with an eye of joy
Too full for continence, that Fate could give
Her darling as a curse; that she may live,
Ere sixteen winters their short course have run,
In agonies of soul to curse that son. 590

 Pray then for daughters, ye wise Mothers! pray;
They shall reward your love, not make ye gray
Before your time with sorrow: they shall give
Ages of peace and comfort; whilst ye live
Make life most truly worth your care, and save, 595
In spite of death, your mem'ries from the grave.

 That sense, with more than manly vigour fraught,
That fortitude of soul, that stretch of thought,
That genius great beyond the narrow bound
Of earth's low walk, that judgment perfect found
When wanted most, that purity of taste 601
Which critics mention by the name of Chaste;
Adorn'd with elegance, that easy flow
Of ready wit which never made a foe;
That face, that form, that dignity, that ease, 605
Those pow'rs of pleasing, with that will to please,
By which Lepel, when in her youthful days,
Ev'n from the currish Pope extorted praise,
We see transmitted in her daughter shine,
And view a new Lepel in Caroline. 610

 Is a son born into this world of wo?
In never-ceasing streams let sorrow flow;

Be from that hour the house with sables hung,
Let lamentations dwell upon thy tongue
Ev'n from the moment that he first began   615
To wail and whine; let him not see a man:
Lock, lock him up, far from the public eye;
Give him no opportunity to buy,
Or to be bought; B——, tho' rich, was sold,
And gave his body up to shame for gold.   620
   Let it be bruited all about the Town
That he is coarse, indelicate, and brown,
An antidote to lust; his face deep scarr'd
With the small-pox, his body maim'd and marr'd,
Ate up with the king's-evil, and his blood   625
Tainted throughout, a thick and putrid flood,
Where dwells corruption, making him all o'er,
From head to foot, a rank and running sore.
Shouldst thou report him as by Nature made
He is undone, and by thy praise betray'd: 630
Give him out fair, lechers, in number more,
More brutal and more fierce, than throng'd the door
Of Lot in Sodom, shall to thine repair,
And force a passage tho' a god is there.
   Let him not have one servant that is male; 635
Where lords are baffled servants oft' prevail.
Some vices they propose, to all agree;
H—— was guilty, but was M—— free?
   Give him no tutor—throw him to a punk,
Rather than trust his morals to a monk——   640

Monks we all know—we who have liv'd at home
From fair report, and travellers who roam
More feelingly—nor trust him to the gown,
'Tis oft' a covering in this vile Town
For base designs: ourselves have liv'd to see   645
More than one parson in the pillory.
Should he have brothers, (image to thy view
A scene which, tho' not public made, is true)
Let not one brother be to t' other known,
Nor let his father sit with him alone;   650
Be all his servants female, young, and fair;
And if the pride of Nature spur thy heir
To deeds of venery, if, hot and wild,
He chance to get some score of maids with child,
Chide, but forgive him; whoredom is a crime   655
Which more at this than any other time
Calls for indulgence, and 'mongst such a race
To have a bastard is some sign of grace.

 Born in such Times, should I sit tamely down,
Suppress my rage, and saunter thro' the Town   660
As one who knew not or who shar'd these crimes?
Should I at lesser evils point my rhymes,
And let this giant sin, in the full eye
Of Observation, pass unwounded by?
Tho' our meek wives passive obedience taught,   665
Patiently bear those wrongs for which they ought,
With the brave spirit of their dams possest,
To plant a dagger in each husband's breast,

To cut off male-increase from this fair isle,
And turn our Thames into another Nile ; 670
Tho' on his Sunday the smug pulpiteer,
Loud 'gainst all other crimes, is silent here,
And thinks himself absolv'd in the pretence
Of decency which, meant for the defence
Of real virtue, and to raise her price, 675
Becomes an agent for the cause of vice;
Tho' the law sleeps, and thro' the care they take
To drug her well may never more awake;
Born in such Times, nor with that patience curst
Which saints may boast of, I must speak or burst.

   But if, too eager in my bold career, 681
Haply I wound the nice and chaster ear,
If, all unguarded, all too rude, I speak,
And call up blushes in the maiden's cheek,
Forgive, ye Fair!—my real motives view, 685
And to forgiveness add your praises too.
For you I write—nor wish a better plan,
The cause of woman is most worthy man—
For you I still will write, nor hold my hand
Whilst there 's one slave of Sodom in the land. 690

   Let them fly far, and sculk from place to place,
Not daring to meet Manhood face to face,
Their steps I'll track, nor yield them one retreat
Where they may hide their heads or rest their feet,
Till God in wrath shall let his vengeance fall, 695
And make a great example of them all,

Bidding in one grand pile this Town expire,
Her tow'rs in dust, her Thames a lake of fire,
Or they (most worth our wish) convinc'd, tho' late,
Of their past crimes and dangerous estate,   700
Pardon of women with repentance buy,
And learn to honour them as much as I.   702

INDEPENDENCE.

Happy the bard (tho' few such bards we find)
Who 'bove controlment dares to speak his mind,
Dares unabash'd in ev'ry place appear,
And nothing fears but what he ought to fear:
Him Fashion cannot tempt, him abject Need 5
Cannot compel, him Pride cannot mislead
To be the slave of Greatness, to strike sail
When, sweeping onward with her peacock's tail,
Quality in full plumage passes by;
He views her with a fix'd contemptuous eye, 10
And mocks the puppet, keeps his own due state,
And is above conversing with the great.
 Perish those slaves, those minions of the quill,
Who have conspir'd to seize that sacred hill
Where the Nine Sisters pour a genuine strain, 15
And sunk the mountain level with the plain;
Who with mean private views and servile art,
No spark of virtue living in their heart,
Have basely turn'd apostates; have debas'd
Their dignity of office; have disgrac'd, 20
Like Eli's sons, the altars where they stand,
And caus'd their name to stink thro' all the land;
Have stoop'd to prostitute their venal pen
For the support of great but guilty men;

Have made the bard, of their own vile accord, 25
Inferior to that thing we call a Lord.
  What is a Lord? Doth that plain simple word
Contain some magic spell? As soon as heard,
Like an alarum bell on Night's dull ear,
Doth it strike louder, and more strong appear 30
Than other words? Whether we will or no,
Thro' Reason's court doth it unquestion'd go
Ev'n on the mention, and of course transmit
Notions of something excellent, of wit
Pleasing tho' keen, of humour free tho' chaste, 35
Of sterling genius with sound judgment grac'd,
Of virtue far above temptation's reach,
And honour which not malice can impeach?
Believe it not—'t was Nature's first intent
Before their rank became their punishment. 40
They should have pass'd for men, nor blush'd to prize
The blessings she bestow'd—She gave them eyes,
And they could see--she gave them ears--they heard--
The instruments of stirring, and they stirr'd—
Like us, they were design'd to eat, to drink, 45
To talk, and (ev'ry now and then) to think;
Till they, by pride corrupted, for the sake
Of singularity disclaim'd that make;
Till they, disdaining Nature's vulgar mode,
Flew off, and struck into another road, 50
More fitting Quality, and to our view
Came forth a species altogether new,

Something we had not known, or could not know,
Like nothing of God's making here below.
Nature exclaim'd with wonder—Lords are things
Which never made by me were made by kings. 56
   A Lord (nor let the honest and the brave,
The true old noble, with the fool and knave
Here mix his fame; curs'd be that thought of mine
Which with a B— and F— should Grafton join) 60
A Lord (nor here let Censure rashly call
My just contempt of some abuse of all,
And, as of late, when Sodom was my theme,
Slander my purpose and my Muse blaspheme,
Because she stops not, rapid in her song, 65
To make exceptions as she goes along,
Tho' well she hopes to find another year
A whole Minority exceptions here)
A mere, mere Lord, with nothing but the name,
Wealth all his worth, and title all his fame, 70
Lives on another man, himself a blank,
Thankless he lives, or must some grandsire thank
For smuggled honours and ill-gotten pelf;
A bard owes all to Nature and himself.
   Gods! how my soul is burnt up with disdain, 75
When I see men, whom Phœbus in his train
Might view with pride, lackey the heels of those
Whom Genius ranks amongst her greatest foes!
And what's the cause? why, these same sons of scorn,
No thanks to them, were to a title born, 80

And could not help it; by Chance hither sent,
And only deities by accident.
Had fortune on our getting chanc'd to shine,
Their birthright honours had been yours or mine.
'Twas a mere random stroke, and should the throne
Eye thee with favour, proud and lordly grown,   86
Thou tho' a bard might'st be their fellow yet;
But Felix never can be made a wit.
No, in good faith—that's one of those few things
Which Fate hath plac'd beyond the reach of kings:
Bards may be lords, but 't is not in the cards,   91
Play how we will, to turn lords into bards.

   A Bard!--a Lord!--Why, let them, hand in hand,
Go forth as friends, and travel thro' the land,
Observe which word the people can digest   95
Most readily, which goes to market best,
Which gets most credit, whether men will trust
A bard because they think he may be just,
Or on a lord will choose to risk their gains,
Tho' privilege in that point still remains.   100

   A Bard!--a Lord!—Let Reason take her scales,
And fairly weigh those words, see which prevails,
Which in the balance lightly kicks the beam,
And which by sinking we the victor deem.

   'Tis done, and Hermes, by command of Jove, 105
Summons a synod in the sacred grove,
Gods throng with gods to take their chairs on high,
And sit in state the senate of the sky,

Whilst in a kind of parliament below
Men stare at those above, and want to know   110
What they're transacting: Reason takes her stand
Just in the midst, a balance in her hand,
Which o'er and o'er she tries, and finds it true;
From either side, conducted full in view,
A man comes forth, of figure strange and queer; 115
We now and then see something like them here.

   The first was meagre, flimsy, void of strength,
But Nature kindly had made up in length
What she in breadth deny'd: erect and proud,
A head and shoulders taller than the crowd,   120
He deem'd them pigmies all: loose hung his skin
O'er his bare bones: his face so very thin,
So very narrow, and so much beat out,
That physiognomists have made a doubt,
Proportion lost, expression quite forgot,   125
Whether it could be call'd a face or not:
At end of it howe'er, unbless'd with beard,
Some twenty fathom length of chin appear'd:
With legs which we might well conceive that Fate
Meant only to support a spider's weight,   130
Firmly he strove to tread, and with a stride,
Which show'd at once his weakness and his pride,
Shaking himself to pieces, seem'd to cry,
Observe, good People! how I shake the sky.

   In his right hand a paper did he hold,   135
On which at large, in characters of gold,

Distinct and plain for those who run to see,
Saint Archibald had wrote L, O, R, D.
This with an air of scorn he from afar
'Twirl'd into Reason's scales, and on that bar, 140
Which from his soul he hated yet admir'd,
Quick turn'd his back, and as he came retir'd.
The judge to all around his name declar'd;
Each goddess titter'd, each god laugh'd, Jove star'd,
And the whole people cry'd, with one accord, 145
Good Heaven bless us all! is that a Lord?

Such was the first---The second was a man
Whom Nature built on quite a diff'rent plan;
A bear whom, from the moment he was born,
His dam despis'd, and left unlick'd in scorn: 150
A Babel which, the pow'r of art outdone,
She could not finish when she had begun:
An utter Chaos, out of which no might
But that of God could strike one spark of light.

Broad were his shoulders, and from blade to blade
A H—— might at full length have laid: 156
Vast were his bones, his muscles twisted strong;
His face was short, but broader than 't was long;
His features, tho' by Nature they were large,
Contentment had contriv'd to overcharge 160
And bury meaning, save that we might spy
Sense low'ring on the penthouse of his eye:
His arms were two twin oaks; his legs so stout
That they might bear a Mansion-house about;

Nor were they, look but at his body there, 165
Design'd by Fate a much less weight to bear.
   O'er a brown cassock which had once been black,
Which hung in tatters on his brawny back,
A sight most strange and awkward to behold,
He threw a covering of blue and gold. 170
Just at that time of life when man by rule,
The fop laid down, takes up the graver fool,
He started up a fop, and, fond of show,
Look'd like another Hercules turn'd beau.
A subject met with only now and then, 175
Much fitter for the pencil than the pen;
Hogarth would draw him (Envy must allow)
Ev'n to the life, was Hogarth living now.
   With such accoutrements, with such a form,
Much like a porpoise just before a storm, 180
Onward he roll'd: a laugh prevail'd around;
Ev'n Jove was seen to simper; at the sound
(Nor was the cause unknown, for from his youth
Himself he studied by the glass of truth) 184
He join'd their mirth; nor shall the gods condemn
If whilst they laugh'd at him he laugh'd at them.
Judge Reason view'd him with an eye of grace,
Look'd thro' his soul, and quite forgot his face,
And from his hand receiv'd, with fair regard
Plac'd in her other scale, the name of Bard. 190
   Then, (for she did as judges ought to do,
She nothing of the case beforehand knew,

Nor wish'd to know; she neverstretch'd the laws,
Nor basely to anticipate a cause
Compell'd solicitors, no longer free,   195
To shew those briefs she had no right to see)
Then she with equal hand her scales held out,
Nor did the cause one moment hang in doubt;
She held her scales out fair to public view,
The Lord, as sparks fly upwards, upwards flew, 200
More light than air, deceitful in the weight;
The Bard preponderating kept his state;
Reason approv'd, and with a voice, whose sound
Shook earth, shook heaven, on the clearest ground
Pronouncing for the Bards a full decree,   205
Cry'd—"Those must honour them who honour me;
They from this present day, where'er I reign,
In their own right precedence shall obtain:
Merit rules here; be it enough that birth
Intoxicates and sways the fools of earth."   210

 Nor think that here, in hatred to a lord,
I've forg'd a tale, or alter'd a record;
Search when you will (I am not now in sport),
You'll find it register'd in Reason's court.

 Nor think that Envy here hath strung my lyre,
That I depreciate what I most admire,   216
And look on titles with an eye of scorn,
Because I was not to a title born.
By Him that made me I am much more proud,
More inly satisfy'd, to have a crowd   220

Point at me as I pass, and cry—" That's he—
A poor but honest bard, who dares be free
Amidst corruption," than to have a train
Of flick'ring levee slaves to make me vain
Of things I ought to blush for; to run, fly, 225
And live but in the motion of my eye;
When I am less than man my faults t'adore,
And make me think that I am something more.
   Recall past times, bring back the days of old,
When the great noble bore his honours bold, 230
And in the face of peril, when he dar'd
Things which his legal bastard, if declar'd
Might well discredit; faithful to his trust,
In the extremest points of justice just,
Well knowing all, and lov'd by all he knew, 235
True to his king, and to his country true;
Honest at court, above the baits of gain,
Plain in his dress, and in his manners plain;
Mod'rate in wealth, gen'rous, but not profuse,
Well worthy riches, for he knew their use; 240
Possessing much, and yet deserving more,
Deserving those high honours which he wore
With ease to all, and in return gain'd fame,
Which all men paid because he did not claim.
When the grim War was plac'd in dread array, 245
Fierce as the lion roaring for his prey,
Or lioness of royal whelps foredone,
In peace as mild as the departing sun,

A gen'ral blessing wheresoe'er he turn'd,
Patron of learning, nor himself unlearn'd: 250
Ever awake at Pity's tender call,
A father of the poor, a friend to all;
Recall such times, and from the grave bring back
A worth like this, my heart shall bend or crack,
My stubborn pride give way, my tongue proclaim,
And ev'ry Muse conspire to swell his fame, 256
Till Envy shall to him that praise allow
Which she cannot deny to Temple now.

   This justice claims, nor shall the bard forget,
Delighted with the task, to pay that debt, 260
To pay it like a man, and in his lays,
Sounding such worth, prove his own right to praise.
But let not Pride and Prejudice misdeem,
And think that empty titles are my theme:
Titles with me are vain and nothing worth; 265
I rev'rence virtue, but I laugh at birth.
Give me a lord that's honest, frank, and brave,
I am his friend, but cannot be his slave;
Tho' none indeed but blockheads would pretend
To make a slave where they may make a friend. 270
I love his virtues, and will make them known,
Confess his rank, but cann't forget my own.
Give me a lord who, to a title born,
Boasts nothing else, I'll pay him scorn with scorn.
What! shall my pride (and pride is virtue here) 275
Tamely make way if such a wretch appear?

Shall I uncover'd stand, and bend my knee
To such a shadow of nobility,
A shred, a remnant? he might rot unknown
For any real merit of his own,   280
And never had come forth to public note
Had he not worn by chance his father's coat.
To think a M—— worth my least regards
Is treason to the majesty of bards.
 By Nature form'd (when for her honour's sake 285
She something more than common strove to make,
When, overlooking each minute defect,
And all too eager to be quite correct,
In her full heat and vigour she impress'd
Her stamp most strongly on the favour'd breast), 290
The bard, (nor think too lightly that I mean
Those little piddling witlings who o'erween
Of their small parts, the Murphys of the stage,
The Masons and the Whiteheads of the age,
Who all in raptures their own works rehearse, 295
And drawl out measur'd prose which they call Verse)
The real bards, whom native genius fires,
Whom ev'ry maid of Castaly inspires,
Let him consider wherefore he was meant,
Let him but answer Nature's great intent,   300
And fairly weigh himself with other men,
Would ne'er debase the glories of his pen,
Would in full state like a true monarch live,
Nor bate one inch of his prerogative.

Methinks I see old Wingate frowning here, 305
(Wingate may in the season be a peer,
Tho' now, against his will, of figures sick,
He's forc'd to diet on arithmetic,
Ev'n whilst he envies ev'ry Jew he meets,
Who cries old clothes to sell about the streets) 310
Methinks (his mind with future honours big,
His Tyburn bob turn'd to a dress'd bag wig)
I hear him cry—"What doth this jargon mean?
Was ever such a damn'd dull blockhead seen?
Majesty—Bard—Prerogative—Disdain 315
Hath got into and turn'd the fellow's brain:
To Bethlem with him—give him whips and straw—
I'm very sensible he's mad in law.
A saucy groom, who trades in reason, thus
To set himself upon a par with us! 320
If this here's suffer'd, and if that there fool
May when he pleases send us all to school,
Why, then our only bus'ness is outright
To take our caps and bid the world good night.
I've kept a bard myself these twenty years, 325
But nothing of this kind in him appears;
He, like a thorough true-bred spaniel, licks
The hand which cuffs him, and the foot which kicks;
He fetches and he carries, blacks my shoes,
Nor thinks it a discredit to his Muse: 330
A creature of the right chameleon hue,
He wears my colours, yellow or true blue,

Just as I wear them: 't is all one to him
Whether I change thro' conscience or thro' whim.
Now this is something like; on such a plan   335
A bard may find a friend in a great man;
But this proud coxcomb—Zounds! I thought that all
Of this queer tribe had been like my old Paul."

 Injurious thought! accursed be the tongue
On which the vile insinuation hung,   340
The heart where 't was engender'd! curs'd be those,
Those bards, who not themselves alone expose,
But me, but all, and make the very name
By which they 're call'd a standing mark of shame!

 Talk not of custom—'t is the coward's plea,   345
Current with fools, but passes not with me;
An old stale trick, which Guilt hath often try'd
By numbers to o'erpow'r the better side.
Why tell me then that from the birth of Rhyme,
No matter when, down to the present time,   350
As by th' original decree of Fate,
Bards have protection sought amongst the great;
Conscious of weakness have apply'd to them
As vines to elms, and twining round their stem
Flourish'd on high? to gain this wish'd support   355
Ev'n Virgil to Mecænas paid his court.
As to the custom, 't is a point agreed,
But 't was a foolish diffidence, not need,
From which it rose; had bards but truly known
That strength which is most properly their own,   360

Volume III.   P

Without a lord, unpropp'd, they might have stood,
And overtopp'd those giants of the wood.
　But why, when present times my care engage,
Must I go back to the Augustan age?
Why, anxious for the living, am I led　　　　365
Into the mansions of the ancient dead?
Can they find patrons no where but at Rome,
And must I seek Mecænas in the tomb?
Name but a Wingate, twenty fools of note
Start up, and from report Mecænas quote;　　370
Under his colours lords are proud to fight,
Forgetting that Mecænas was a knight;
They mention him, as if to use his name
Was in some measure to partake his fame,
Tho' Virgil, was he living, in the street　　　375
Might rot for them, or perish in the Fleet.
See how they redden and the charge disclaim—
Virgil, and in The Fleet—forbid it, Shame!
Hence, ye vain Boasters! to The Fleet repair,
And ask, with blushes ask, if Lloyd is there.　380
　Patrons in days of yore were men of sense,
Were men of taste, and had a fair pretence
To rule in letters—some of them were heard
To read off hand, and never spell a word:
Some of them, too, to such a monstrous height　385
Was learning risen, for themselves could write,
And kept their secretaries, as the great
Do many other foolish things, for state.

Our patrons are of quite a diff'rent strain,
With neither sense nor taste; against the grain 390
They patronize for fashion's sake—no more—
And keep a bard just as they keep a whore.
M——————— (on such occasion I am loth
To name the dead) was a rare proof of both.
Some of them would be puzzled ev'n to read, 395
Nor could deserve their clergy by their creed:
Others can write, but such a Pagan hand,
A Willes should always at our elbow stand:
Many, if begg'd, a chancellor of right
Would order into keeping at first sight. 400
Those who stand fairest to the public view
Take to themselves the praise to others due,
They rob the very 'spital, and make free
With those, alas! who 've least to spare—We see
——————— hath not had a word to say 405
Since winds and waves bore Singlespeech away.

 Patrons in days of yore, like patrons now,
Expected that the bard should make his bow
At coming in, and ev'ry now and then
Hint to the world that they were more than men;
But, like the patrons of the present day, 411
They never bilk'd the poet of his pay.
Virgil lov'd rural ease, and, far from harm,
Mecænas fix'd him in a neat snug farm,
Where he might free from trouble pass his days 415
In his own way, and pay his rent in praise.

P ij

Horace lov'd wine, and thro' his friend at court
Could buy it off the key in ev'ry port:
Horace lov'd mirth, Mecænas lov'd it too;
They met, they laugh'd, as Gay and I may do, 420
Nor in those moments paid the least regard
To which was minister and which was bard.

   Not so our patrons—grave as grave can be,
They know themselves, they keep up dignity.
Bards are a forward race, nor is it fit 425
That men of fortune rank with men of wit:
Wit if familiar made will find her strength—
'Tis best to keep her weak and at arm's length.
'Tis well enough for bards if patrons give,
From hand to mouth, the scanty means to live. 430
Such is their language, and their practice such;
They promise little, and they give not much.
Let the weak bard, with prostituted strain,
Praise that proud Scot whom all good men disdain;
What's his reward? why, his own fame undone,
He may obtain a patent for the run 436
Of his lord's kitchen, and have ample time,
With offal fed, to court the cook in rhyme;
Or (if he strives true patriots to disgrace)
May at the second table get a place, 440
With somewhat greater slaves allow'd to dine,
And play at crambo o'er his gill of wine.

   And are there bards who, on Creation's file,
Stand rank'd as men, who breathe in this fair isle

The air of freedom, with so little gall, 445
So low a spirit, prostrate thus to fall
Before these idols, and without a groan
Bear wrongs might call forth murmurs from a stone?
Better and much more noble to abjure
The sight of men, and in some cave, secure 450
From all the outrages of Pride, to feast
On Nature's sallads, and be free at least.
Better, (tho' that, to say the truth, is worse
Than almost any other modern curse)
Discard all sense, divorce the thankless Muse, 455
Critics commence, and write in the Reviews;
Write without tremor; Griffiths* cannot read;
No fool can fail where Langhorne can succeed.

  But (not to make a brave and honest pride
Try those means first she must disdain when try'd)
There are a thousand ways, a thousand arts, 461
By which, and fairly, men of real parts
May gain a living, gain what Nature craves;
Let those who pine for more live and be slaves.
Our real wants in a small compass lie, 465
But lawless appetite with eager eye,
Kept in a constant fever, more requires,
And we are burnt up with our own desires.
Hence our dependence, hence our slav'ry, springs:
Bards if contented are as great as kings. 470

    * Publisher of The Monthly Review.

Ourselves are to ourselves the cause of ill;
We may be independent if we will.
The man who suits his spirit to his state
Stands on an equal footing with the great:
Moguls themselves are not more rich, and he   475
Who rules the English nation not more free.
Chains were not forg'd more durable and strong
For bards than others, but they've worn them long,
And therefore wear them still; they've quite forgot
What freedom is, and therefore prize her not.   480
Could they, tho' in their sleep, could they but know
The blessings which from Independence flow;
Could they but have a short and transient gleam
Of liberty, tho' 't was but in a dream,
They would no more in bondage bend their knee, 485
But once made freemen would be always free.
The Muse, if she one moment freedom gains,
Can never more submit to sing in chains.
Bred in a cage, far from the feather'd throng,
The bird repays his keeper with his song;   490
But if some playful child sets wide the door
Abroad he flies, and thinks of home no more,
With love of liberty begins to burn,
And rather starves than to his cage return.

    Hail, Independence!—by true reason taught 495
How few have known and priz'd thee as they ought!
Some give thee up for riot; some, like boys,
Resign thee in their childish moods for toys;

Ambition some, some avarice, misleads,
And in both cases Independence bleeds.   500
Abroad in quest of thee how many roam,
Nor know they had thee in their reach at home!
Some, tho' about their paths, their beds about,
Have never had the sense to find thee out:
Others, who know of what they are possest,   505
Like fearful misers lock thee in a chest,
Nor have the resolution to produce,
In these bad times, and bring thee forth for use.
Hail, Independence!—tho' thy name's scarce known,
Tho' thou, alas! art out of fashion grown,   510
Tho' all despise thee, I will not despise,
Nor live one moment longer than I prize
Thy presence, and enjoy. By angry Fate [late,
Bow'd down, and almost crush'd, thou cam'st, tho'
Thou cam'st upon me like a second birth,   515
And made me know what life was truly worth.
Hail, Independence! never may my cot,
Till I forget thee, be by thee forgot:
Thither, O thither! oftentimes repair;
Cotes, whom thou lovest too, shall meet thee there:
All thoughts but what arise from joy give o'er; 521
Peace dwells within, and Law shall guard the door.
  O'erweening Bard! Law guard thy door! what law?
The law of England—To control and awe
Those saucy hopes, to strike that spirit dumb, 525
Behold in state Administration come!

Why, let her come, in all her terrors too;
I dare to suffer all she dares to do.
I know her malice well, and know her pride,
I know her strength, but will not change my side.
This melting mass of flesh she may control   531
With iron ribs, she cannot chain my soul.
No—to the last resolv'd her worst to bear,
I'm still at large, and independent there.

Where is this minister? where is the band   535
Of ready slaves who at his elbow stand
To hear and to perform his wicked will?
Why for the first time are they slow to ill?
When some grand act 'gainst law is to be done
Doth —— sleep? doth blood-hound —— run   540
To L——, and worry those small deer,
When he might do more precious mischief here?
Doth —— turn tail? doth he refuse to draw
Illegal warrants, and to call them Law?
Doth —— at G——d kick'd, from G——d run,
With that cold lump of unbak'd dough his son,
And, his more honest rival Ketch to cheat,   546
Purchase a burial-place where three ways meet?
Believe it not; —— is —— still,
And never sleeps when he should wake to ill: 550
—— doth lesser mischiefs, by the by,
The great ones till the term in petto lie:
—— lives, and, to the strictest justice true,
Scorns to defraud the hangman of his due.

O my poor Country!—weak, and overpower'd
By thine own sons—ate to the bone—devour'd 556
By vipers, which, in thine own entrails bred,
Prey on thy life, and with thy blood are fed,
With unavailing grief thy wrongs I see,
And for myself not feeling feel for thee. 560
I grieve, but cann't despair—for, lo! at hand
Freedom presents a choice but faithful band
Of loyal patriots; men who greatly dare
In such a noble cause: men fit to bear 564
The weight of empires; Fortune, Rank, and Sense,
Virtue and Knowledge, leagu'd with Eloquence,
March in their ranks; Freedom from file to file
Darts her delighted eye, and with a smile
Approves her honest sons, whilst down her cheek,
As 't were by stealth (her heart too full to speak), 570
One tear in silence creeps, one honest tear,
And seems to say, Why is not Granby here?

O ye brave Few! in whom we still may find
A love of virtue, freedom, and mankind,
Go forth—in majesty of wo array'd, 575
See! at your feet your Country kneels for aid,
And (many of her children traitors grown)
Kneels to those sons she still can call her own;
Seeming to breathe her last in ev'ry breath,
She kneels for freedom, or she begs for death— 580
Fly then each duteous son, each English chief,
And to your drooping parent bring relief.

Go forth—nor let the Siren voice of Ease
Tempt ye to sleep whilst tempests swell the seas;
Go forth— nor let Hypocrisy, whose tongue 585
With many a fair, false, fatal art is hung,
Like Bethel's fawning prophet, cross your way,
When your great errand brooks not of delay;
Nor let vain Fear, who cries to all she meets,
Trembling and pale—A lion in the streets— 590
Damp your free spirits; let not threats affright,
Nor bribe corrupt, nor flatteries delight.
Be as one man—Concord success ensures—
There's not an English heart but what is yours.
Go forth— and Virtue, ever in your sight, 595
Shall be your guide by day, your guard by night—
Go forth—the champions of your native land,
And may the battle prosper in your hand—
It may, it must—ye cannot be withstood—
Be your hearts honest as your cause is good. 600

THE POETRY PROFESSORS.*

OLD England has not lost her pray'r,
And George the Good has got an heir;
A royal babe, a Prince of Wales;
—Poets! I pity all your nails—
What reams of paper will be spoil'd,   5
What graduses be daily soil'd,
By inky fingers, greasy thumbs,
Hunting the word that never comes!
 Now academics pump their wits,
And lash in vain their lazy tits;   10
In vain they whip, and lash, and spur,
The callous jades will never stir,
Nor can they reach Parnassus' hill,
Try ev'ry method which they will:
Nay, should the tits get on for once,   15
Each rider is so grave a dunce
That, as I've heard good judges say,
'T is ten to one they 'd lose their way;
Tho' not one wit bestrides the back   20
Of youthful drudge, ycleped Hack,
But fine-bred things of mettled blood,
Pick'd from Apollo's royal stud,

 * This poem was not published in Churchill's name, but is admitted by many to be his, and therefore it was thought proper to annex it to this edition of his Works.

Greek, Roman, nay, Arabian steeds,
Or those our mother-country breeds.
Some ride ye in and ride ye out, 25
And to come home go round about,
Nor on the green sward nor the road,
And that I think they call an Ode:
Some take the pleasant country air,
And smack their whips and drive a pair. 30
Each horse with bells which chink and chime,
And so they march—and that is rhyme:
Some copy with prodigious skill
The figures of a butter bill,
Which with great folks of erudition 35
Shall pass for Coptic or Phœnician;
While some, as patriot love prevails,
To compliment a Prince of Wales,
Salute the royal babe in Welsh,
And send forth gutt'rals like a belch. 40
    What pretty things imagination
Will fritter out in adulation!
The Pagan gods shall visit earth
To triumph in a Christian's birth,
While Classic poets, pure and chaste, 45
Of trim and academic taste,
Shall lug them in by head and shoulders,
To be or speakers or beholders.
Mars shall present him with a lance
To humble Spain and conquer France; 50

The Graces, buxom, blithe, and gay,
Shall at his cradle dance the Hay;
And Venus with her train of Loves
Shall bring a thousand pair of doves
To bill, to coo, to whine, to squeak,   55
Thro' all the dialects of Greek.
How many swains of Classic breed
Shall deftly tune their oaten reed,
And bring their Doric nymphs to Town,
To sing their measures up and down,   6
In notes alternate, clear, and sweet,
Like ballad-singers in a street!
While those who grasp at reputation,
From imitating imitation,
Shall hunt each cranny, nook, and creek,   65
From precious fragments in the Greek,
And rob the 'spital and the waste
For sense, and sentiment, and taste.
    What Latin hodge podge, Grecian hash,
With Hebrew roots and English trash,   70
Shall academic cooks produce
For present show and future use!
Fellows who 've soak'd away their knowledge
In sleepy residence at college;
Whose lives are like a stagnant pool,   75
Muddy and placid, dull and cool,
Mere drinking, eating, eating, drinking,
With no impertinence of thinking;

Volume III.   Q

Who lack no farther erudition
Than just to set an imposition, 80
To cramp, demolish, and dispirit,
Each true-begotten child of Merit;
Censors who, in the day's broad light,
Punish the vice they act at night;
Whose charity with self begins, 85
Nor covers others venial sins;
But that their feet may safely tread
Take up hypocrisy instead,
As knowing that must always hide
A multitude of sins beside; 90
Whose rusty wit is at a stand
Without a fresh man at their hand,
(Whose service must of course create
The just return of sevenfold hate)
Lord! that such good and useful men 95
Should ever turn to books agen!

   Yet matter must be gravely plann'd,
And syllables on fingers scann'd,
And racking pangs rend lab'ring head,
Till Lady Muse is gone to bed; 100
What hunting, changing, toiling, sweating,
To bring the useful epithet in!

   Where the crampt measure kindly shows
It will be verse but should be prose;
So when 't is neither light nor dark,
To 'prentice spruce or lawyer's clerk,

The nymph who takes her nightly stand
At some sly corner in the Strand,
Plump in the chest, tight in the boddice,
Seems to the eye a perfect goddess, 110
But canvass'd more minutely o'er,
Turns out an old, stale, batter'd, whore.
   Yet must these sons of gowned ease,
Proud of the plumage of degrees,
Forsake their apathy awhile, 115
To figure in the Roman style,
And offer incense at the shrine
Of Latin poetry divine.
   Upon the throne, the goddess sits,
Surrounded by her bulky wits; 120
Fabricius, Cooper, Calepine,
Ainsworthus, Faber, Constantine,
And he who like Dodona spoke,
De sacra quercu, Holyoak;
These are her counsellors of state, 125
Men of much words, and wits of weight.
Here Gradus, full of phrases clever,
Lord of her treasury for ever,
With lib'ral hand his bounty deals,
Sir Cento Keeper of the Seals. 130
Next to the person of the queen
Old Madam Prosody is seen,
Talking incessant, altho' dumb,
Upon her fingers to her thumb.

And all around her portraits hung 135
Of heroes in the Latin tongue,
Italian, English, German, French,
Who most laboriously intrench
In deep parade of language dead,
What would not in their own be read 140
Without impeachment of that taste
Which Latin idiom turns to chaste.
Santolius here, whose flippant joke
Sought refuge in a Roman cloke,
With dull Commirius at his side, 145
In all the pomp of Jesuit pride:
Menage the pedant figur'd there,
A trifler with a solemn air;
And there, in loose unseemly view,
The graceless easy Loveling too. 150
   'Tis here grave poets urge their claim
For some thin blast of tiny fame;
Here bind their temples drunk with praise,
With half a sprig of wither'd bays.
   O Poet! if that honour'd name 155
Befits such idle childish aim,
If Virgil ask thy sacred care,
If Horace charm thee, oh! forbear
To spoil, with sacrilegious hand,
The glories of the Classic land, 160
Nor sow thy dowlas on the satin
Of their pure uncorrupted Latin.

Better be native in thy verse——
What is Fingal but genuine Erse?
Which all sublime sonorous flows, 165
Like Hervey's Thoughts, in drunken prose.
   Hail, Scotland! hail! to thee belong
All pow'rs, but most the pow'rs of song;
Whether the rude unpolish'd Erse
Stalk in the buckram prose or verse, 170
Or Bonny Ramsay please thee mo',
Who sang sae sweetly a' his wo.
If aught, and say who knows so well?
The secondsighted Muse can tell,
The happy lairds shall laugh and sing 175
When England's Genius droops his wing;
So shall thy soil new wealth disclose,
So thy own Thistle choke the Rose.
   But what comes here? methinks I see
A walking university. 180
See how they press to cross the Tweed,
And strain their limbs with eager speed!
While Scotland, from her fertile shore,
Cries, "On, my sons! return no more."
   Hither they haste with willing mind, 185
Nor cast one longing look behind,
On ten-toe carriage to salute
The King and Queen and Earl of Bute.
No more the gallant northern sons
Spout forth their strings of Latin puns, 190

Nor course all languages to frame
The quibble suited to their name,
As when their ancestors bevers'd
That glorious Stewart James 'The First,
But with that elocution's grace, 195
That Oriental flashy lace,
Which the fam'd Irish Tommy Puff
Would sow on sentimental stuff,
'Twang with a sweet pronunciation
The flow'rs of bold imagination. 200
Macpherson leads the flaming van,
Laird of the new Fingalian clan,
While Jacky Home brings up the rear,
With new-got pension, neat and clear,
Three hundred English pounds a-year, 205
While sister Peg, our ancient friend,
Sends Macs and Donalds without end:
To George a while they tune their lays,
Then all their choral voices raise
To heap their panegyric wit on 210
Th' illustrious chief and our North Briton.
 Hail to the Thane whose patriot skill
Can break all nations to his will!
Master of sciences and arts,
Mecænas to all men of parts, 215
Whose fost'ring hand and ready wit
Shall find us all in places fit;

So shall thy friends no longer roam,
But change to meet a settled home.
Hail, mighty Thane! for Scotland born,   220
To fill her almost empty horn;
Hail to thy ancient glorious stem,
Not they from kings, but kings from them!   223

The six following lines are not inserted in any former edition of Mr. Churchill's works, though well known to be written by him.

PROUD Buckingham, for law too mighty grown,
A patriot dagger prob'd, and from the throne
Sever'd its minion. In succeeding times
May all those fav'rites who adopt his crimes
Partake his fate, and ev'ry Villiers feel
The keen deep searchings of a Felton's steel!   6

CONTENTS.

THE DUELLIST. IN THREE BOOKS.

	Page
Book I.	5
Book II.	15
Book III.	26

GOTHAM. IN THREE BOOKS.

Book I.	43
Book II.	61
Book III.	86

The Prophecy of Famine. A Scots Pastoral. Inscribed to John Wilkes, Esq.	110
The Times,	131
Independence,	157
The Poetry Professors,	179
Lines not in any former edition,	187

THE END.

www.ingramcontent.com/pod-product-compliance
Lightning Source LLC
Chambersburg PA
CBHW030434190426
43202CB00036B/176